Managing Quality Cultural Tourism

The Heritage: Care–Preservation–Management programme has been designed to serve the needs of the museum and heritage community worldwide. It publishes books and information services for professional museum and heritage workers, and for all the organisations that service the museum community.

Editor-in-chief: Andrew Wheatcroft

Architecture in Conservation:
Managing developments at historic sites
James Strike

The Development of Costume
Naomi Tarrant

Forward Planning: *A handbook of business, corporate and development planning for museums and galleries*
Edited by Timothy Ambrose and Sue Runyard

The Handbook for Museums
Gary Edson and David Dean

Heritage Gardens: *Care, conservation and management*
Sheena Mackellar Goulty

Heritage and Tourism *in 'the global village'*
Priscilla Boniface and Peter J. Fowler

The Industrial Heritage: *Managing resources and uses*
Judith Alfrey and Tim Putnam

Museum Basics
Timothy Ambrose and Crispin Paine

Museum Exhibition: *Theory and practice*
David Dean

Museum, Media, Message
Edited by Eilean Hooper-Greenhill

Museum Security and Protection:
A handbook for cultural heritage institutions
ICOM and ICMS

Museums 2000: *Politics, people, professionals and profit*
Edited by Patrick J. Boylan

Museums and the Shaping of Knowledge
Eilean Hooper-Greenhill

Museums and their Visitors
Eilean Hooper-Greenhill

Museums without Barriers: *A new deal for disabled people*
Fondation de France and ICOM

The Past in Contemporary Society: Then/Now
Peter J. Fowler

The Representation of the Past:
Museums and heritage in the post-modern world
Kevin Walsh

Towards the Museum of the Future: *New European perspectives*
Edited by Roger Miles and Lauro Zavala

Managing Quality Cultural Tourism

Priscilla Boniface

ROUTLEDGE

London and New York

First published 1995
by Routledge
2 Park Square, Milton Park, Abingdon, Oxon, OX14 4RN
Simultaneously published in the USA and Canada
by Routledge
270 Madison Ave, New York NY 10016

Transferred to Digital Printing 2007

© 1995 Priscilla Boniface

Typeset in Sabon by Florencetype Ltd, Stoodleigh, Devon

British Library Cataloguing in Publication Data
A catalogue record for this book is available from the
British Library

Library of Congress Cataloguing in Publication Data
A catalogue record for this book has been requested

ISBN 0-415-09985-4

Publisher's Note
The publisher has gone to great lengths to ensure the quality of
this reprint but points out that some imperfections in the
original may be apparent

Contents

Preface

The aim of this book is to set out and describe matters and issues concerning the pursuit of achieving happy heritage visits by those managing quality cultural tourism. In both structure and content the book has to the fore the perceived needs of teachers, students and practitioners in the general fields of tourism and leisure, heritage and cultural resource management.

The concern will be to highlight (a) circumstances in society in general, (b) circumstances which, in particular, concern cultural tourism and (c) circumstances which pertain to a site or item, or group of sites or items, which together condition what would be the appropriate tourism response in each individual situation. In using the word 'appropriate', my meaning is 'that which is most suitable in all the prevailing circumstances'. The word is central to the book. With this assessment of sites in their context, I shall suggest ways, means and alternative methods for them to be managed to achieve a quality cultural tourism product.

Culture is very much tourism's main attraction. Without culture to make the difference, every place would seem blandly the same. Without a belief in new or different sensations and benefits at journey's end, what incentive would there be for any of us to make a visit that is discretionary in type? With no destination dissimilar, a journey would hardly ever be deemed so desirable as to be 'necessary'; and what position would the tourism industry be left in then, poor thing? Without their different cultural heritages, therefore, places around the world would have little to offer that would attract for purposes of tourism.

Despite a situation of world recession at the time of writing, tourism continues on the path predicted for it of becoming the number one industry in the world by the millennium. In this circumstance, presenters, understandably, will increasingly want more and more to use more and more cultural heritage for *their* purpose. Many people in many guises will meanwhile expand upon use of the cultural heritage as consumers. The product, focus of both groups, subject of much increased use, may be under many, varied and great pressures. There is growing concern in various quarters and places, both professional and lay, about how to meet the tourism demands of the cultural heritage appropriately, without irrevocable and unreasonable damage to the primary resource.

A fundamental difficulty in trying to satisfy the needs of a site or item, its presenter and its user, is that the needs of the last two are likely to be essentially short term, whereas those of a site or item, for its continued preservation, require gratification on a continuous, long-term basis. In theory, either visitor or presenter can move on elsewhere if a chosen heritage resource is exhausted or eradicated through over-use and exploitation, but once that primary historical resource is damaged or lost, it can then at best only be repaired, or re-created in replica.

Accepting that cultural tourism is a boom, how, if it all, can it be made a boon for everyone concerned? My attempt to answer that question is the subject of this book. I begin from the premise that if we all want to join in the activity of cultural tourism in some manner, on the grounds of practicality alone we can no longer just continue doing so in the same way: the resource alone cannot stand it. On the one hand, we need to recognize that we cannot automatically expect to engage in traditional cultural tourism as we want to, when we want to and how we want to. On the other hand, we need to identify more closely what are the various requirements of cultural tourism, with the purpose of then finding a greater range of types of ways, both old and new, of meeting them appropriately.

My starting point is that, whether we like it or not, cultural tourism is here to stay and set to grow, and that, therefore, we had better get down to seeing that this activity is characterized, throughout, by the best conduct possible.

As more and more of us come to consider we have right of access to the world's cultural heritage, we create for ourselves a challenge in handling a situation of epic proportions. The only response with a hope of meeting that challenge, I believe, is management of a very high order and quality. The focus of this book is to suggest ways towards management of this type – management which will most likely meet the needs of the heritage item, its user and its presenter. Heritage tourism is a three-way relationship, between a site, its presenter and its audience. My intention is to suggest how this relationship may be made as happy and suitable as possible for all three, in all the prevailing circumstances.

At the start of the book, in Part 1, I shall outline the general situation of cultural tourism, before I seek in Part 2 to identify the various needs of culture of the three groups: the user, the presenter and the item of culture/heritage itself. In Part 3 I shall suggest ways in which the various, often conflicting needs may be met most suitably. I shall mention examples, good, bad and ugly to illustrate points. In Part 4 I shall present my conclusion. My aim throughout is to show how that felicitous event the happy heritage visit, may be achieved and to define attitudes, types and methods of approach to managing quality cultural tourism.

Acknowledgements

People, places, matters and media items, around the world, serve to stimulate my thoughts. In the preparation of this book, that all these are source both for encouraging ideas and, in the instance of the media, of material for examples, is obvious. I would therefore like to say a huge thank you for this. For inspiration by his breadth of knowledge and his generosity in sharing it, deserving of special mention is Kevin Robins, Reader in Cultural Geography at the University of Newcastle upon Tyne. The energetic and steadfast enthusiasm for the project of Andrew Wheatcroft, my editor, whose was the original idea for the book, has been enormously helpful, and he has firmly, kindly and positively kept me from straying over-far from that first concept. Closest encouragement has come from Professor Peter Fowler.

I am deeply grateful to you all.

About the book for teaching purposes

As I mentioned in the Preface, this book is structured with a view to the uses that teachers and students may wish to make of it.

The text of the book is arranged so that the subject is introduced in general by considering the situation of cultural tourism. Then the principal elements of the cultural tourism product are looked at, followed by an analysis of the component needs and aims of cultural tourism and how they can be met, and thereafter there is a conclusion.

Following each chapter are two additional items: one outlines the chapter's main *Issues and questions*; the other provides suggestions for *Further reading*.

At the end of the book are: a Glossary; Notes, listed by chapter; and a general Select bibliography. The Index itemizes items, issues and places.

The book can be used for:

a)   teaching for the tourism and leisure and heritage professions;
b)   for higher education in universities and technical training colleges over a range of humanities and social science disciplines and vocational subjects;
c)   for secondary education at school at National Curriculum Key Stage 4 level.

Part 1
Introduction

1.1 The situation of cultural tourism

1.1

The situation of cultural tourism

The intercultural tourism ideal

It could be asked who of any among the community of the world would dare even to consider for a second that tourism, and more especially cultural tourism, should be exclusive? Our society is global but it is composed of myriad different cultures. To live together harmoniously we need to:

i)   know about,
ii) respect,

and, if possible,

iii) understand

each other's ways of life. Selective denial of such knowledge, respect and understanding, therefore, would be unfair and unsuitable. Problematic though it may be in practice – and often it is very, very difficult, sometimes impossible – we must surely set out to find a solution to the many and various problems attendant upon acceptance of the point from a place of departure which says this: that, in theory at least, provided other criteria are met, there should be equal right of opportunity of access, or where unavoidable non-access, to any part of the cultural heritage.

General methods of approach to the management of cultural tourism

Tourism is a massive ingredient of the modern world. We live in the modern world, and we must seek **modern methods** to make tourism work. Trying to apply methods from a different age is unlikely to be successful in our times. Approaches such as 'green' and 'eco' tourism, founded on precepts of being gentle to people and places, are fine, but on their own, and without their being given contemporary interpretation and application, such endeavours cannot hope to meet cultural tourism needs and demands on the scale and complexity of the present day. Methods for our times are required, fuelled with all the humanity and holism learnt from earlier ages and from less complex societies, but created nevertheless for us now. Our approach needs to be humanistic and holistic while, at the same time, the most up-to-date and sophisticated technology is deployed to achieve aims.

The cultural tourism spread across the world: ranges of, and reasons for, the variety of visitor loads

In many places across the world, many cultural tourism attractions are suffering visitor overload already, while others are visited to capacity. Elsewhere, and often in these very same overall locations, there are cultural items which are intended to attract visitors yet, for a reason or reasons, they are not fulfilling that role with much success. In other places cultural tourism has scarcely, or not at all, been begun as an industry or activity.

In the situation so described, it is not difficult to see that the tourism aims for one group are scarcely likely to be the same as another.

1 Cultural sites: World Heritage Sites as example

World Heritage Sites might be thought, by their nature, to fall entirely into the first category described above – to be over-visited or visited to capacity – and certainly many are, such as Mesa Verde, Mont St Michel, the Pyramids (at least until the radical change in situation brought about through tourists in Egypt becoming a focus of religious fundamentalists' attention), the Tower of London and the Taj Mahal. Yet, it is not this simple, even with a World Heritage Site.

First, a **total global heritage overview** is precluded because not every country in the world is a signatory to the World Heritage Convention. A country which has put forward its site to the World Heritage Committee for inclusion on the World Heritage List in the first instance, for very good reasons of its own, may know the Site is under stress but, for economic reasons, not care to admit it. In other instances, one part of a Site may be worn down while another may be almost deserted, possessing the capacity to bear plenty more visits: either way, local people involved in associated entrepreneurial activity may be 'crying out' for more people to visit, while other disinterested locals might want to be left in peace. The physical state of what remains of the original fabric of the relevant portion of the – immensely long overall – Great Wall of China, where VIPs tend to be taken for valuable photo-opportunities, is scarcely likely to be a first concern of host or visitor. Here, *looking* good is the prime requirement.

2 *Why visitors are brought to a site*

Among the reasons for promoting, or not promoting, one attraction at the expense of another, those of **economic** and/or **political** or **social prestige** are usually to the fore. As will be demonstrated, however, there are also many other possible reasons. And, as will be shown, all the promotion in the world may not be able to overcome a basic element of 'turn off' to tourists about a site.

3 *Why visitors are motivated to visit a site*

The explosion in tourism in general is principally rooted in better communications, increased affluence and more leisure. In regard to what is seen as *cultural* tourism, as was suggested in the Preface, any tourism, even tourism ostensibly of the 'sun and sand' variety, or, for that matter, with the purpose of 'visiting a friend up the road', would have little power of attraction without the presence of some alien culture, of **differentness**. Without this, what would be the point of leaving home?

4 *The needs of the visitor; the presenter; the cultural site/item*

The variety of needs which may be the impulse for cultural tourism on behalf of visitor and presenter will be looked at more closely in Chapters 2.1 and 2.2 respectively. The needs of the object of attention, the cultural site or item, will be addressed in Chapter 2.3.

Cultural tourism: an appraisal

Culture has terrific power. We stand in awe of what our fellow men have done, and can do. It inspires us to do things ourselves, things that we might otherwise never have thought of doing or felt capable of attempting. We 'feed' off other people's culture for our own ends. We hope our culture does the same for them. A visit to a cultural site, if it goes 'right', can be a very strengthening experience. It has the capacity to disturb us, and if it does this it is not necessarily a bad thing.

Tourism is now integral to modern life: not merely in financial terms, such as the assessment of the WTTC that by 1990 tourism accounted for 5.5 per cent of the world gross national product,[1] but in much deeper, more radical ways as well. As Deyan Sudjic has unequivocally pronounced in his book *The 100 Mile City*,[2] 'As a force for social change, tourism has had an impact of the same order as the industrial revolution. In less than three decades, tourism has transformed the way the world looks and works.'

The first and only basis for consideration of the most appropropriate way to conduct cultural tourism is a recognition that the agenda must be determined, and then implemented, globally, on the basis of an acceptance of our complete interdependence. To the question 'Western vs Non-Western: Whose Culture will Save the Environment?'[3] which UNESCO posed for its International Symposium on Culture and Environment in Indonesia, the answer would be that there can only be one answer and that is 'both, *together*'. This is, of course, much easier said than done but the existence, and their concern in this area, of supra-organizations such as UNESCO, ICOMOS, ICOM, WTO and the WTTC, and the staging of such events as the global Earth Summit in Rio, are indicative that, whether in theory or not, at least acceptance of the principle is widespread. Putting noble thoughts and aims into action, however, perhaps because of other consequences regarded as more immediately dire at the local level, may militate against the necessary 'follow through'. Emblem to such difficulty is the global split revealed at the 1992 Rio conference: and much is the sympathy for hard-pressed areas, desperately trying to solve urgent basic problems of human need, who see conservation, preservation and gentle tourism as luxuries they cannot afford. As was opined by François Ascher in a UNESCO publication,[4] 'Tourism is an economic activity which may be said to trade in the cultural and natural heritage of countries. It thus involves an inseparable combination of economic and socio-cultural problems and immediately raises the issue of development options.'

While not all the world's population yet travel physically, we are a stage when most places are, to a degree, visited by outsiders. Viewed from some perspectives, this can produce unfortunate inequalities: some people can enjoy the life of a global citizen, while others may rarely, or never, go further than their own backyard. However, when considering how to manage cultural tourism, that entity is being viewed in its widest sense, since it is regarded as essential to the search and discovery of an appropriate agenda for cultural tourism that this be done.

The 'think global, act local' mantra has permeated well certain strata of society, including many of the media. This can tend, due to the high visibility character of their opinion, to lend the impression that the point has been taken universally. It is debatable whether, even in this day and age, everyone knows what is said in such media-orientated circles, and if they do they will not necessarily share their viewpoint. For reasons such as ignorance, self-interest or selfishness, some portions of world society are still likely only to think, as well as to act, local. Even well-meaning pan-national or cultural gatherings can end with the victory of individual interest against that of the group as a whole.

So tourism, as a global industry, is liable to be influenced by the forces of, **politics, economics and culture**. For the practice of cultural tourism, the Preface outlined the suggested aims for achievement in terms of suitable conduct, by the meeting of the three needs of:

i)   an item of heritage,
ii)   its presenter,
iii) its audience.

As has been indicated above, those needs will be discussed in separate chapters.

Main methods of use

Here will be outlined what are considered to be the three main tools or methods for use. First, though, what is extremely obvious should nevertheless be stressed. This is that, in the case of a world industry of massive complexity, there can be no easy answers to how it can be run appropriately. The purpose of this book is to suggest the principal routes of approach, those which, it is thought, are most likely to lead to the most success.

One way is, quite simply, the **traditional style of management, but done better.** Another is a **different style of management,** a shift in perspective in other words. The last way is one upon which I place the most emphasis, not just because I believe it holds out the best hope of ameliorating cultural tourism's current situation of crisis, but because it seeks to solve a contemporary problem through contemporary means. By nature, instinct and intellect, I am impelled to think that, in the conduct of cultural tourism, provided it is used both subject to and harnessed with human sensitivity and creativity, and in alignment and harmony as far as possible with nature, **technology represents the best route forward** and the most appropriate way to proceed. We need to be imaginative and innovative.

Possibly few people would guess correctly which was the most visited cultural site in the European Community in 1988. The Tower of London, perhaps? Versailles? The Louvre? No, it was the Pompidou Centre, by a margin of 3.9 million visits over its nearest rival, the Louvre, with 4 million visits. This is interesting and seems to suggest various things, not least about visitors' motivations in regard to the cultural heritage. The subject of the Pompidou Centre is discussed in Chapter 2.1. Indicative, meanwhile, and very relevant in considering the most appropriate way of managing the cultural heritage for tourism, is that Richard Rogers – a leading world architect who, with the Italian, Renzo Piano, designed the Pompidou Centre – should hold the opinion that 'The 20th century has seen an explosion of new ideas and technologies, but their emancipatory potential has rarely been fulfilled.'[5] Interestingly, Rogers is the architect of the Council of Europe's new Court of Human Rights.

As I have indicated already, I favour the modernist approach. In ensuing chapters I shall follow a three-pronged line of enquiry, giving consideration to all three action options that I put forward. Nevertheless, I think that of these three, the traditional and green options have in-built limitations. Again, Rogers has relevant words to say on our subject, on this occasion in the context of adopting a traditional approach: 'There are important, visual, technical and social lessons to be learnt from the past, but merely copying the outward forms belittles history.'[6] Indeed; and what was right for a situation in one age is scarcely likely to be suitable, unaltered, for another.

I find a similar difficulty with the green ethos, having a problem seeing how what I consider to be essentially a 'hark-back' technique can be applied to what is such a fundamentally huge and contemporary situation. The greening of the world, however laudable an aim, and while it may well represent in theory the best answer to our massive global problems, including those of cultural tourism, has, I believe, a certain in-built capacity for failure because the solutions it proposes are not of our time. They are not attuned to the spirit of our times, and thus they can never truly enter the contemporary psyche. The general silence post-Rio, although much seems to be being done quietly behind the scenes, activating the Agenda 21 strategy for sustainable development, for example, does perhaps rather indicate commitment to fine principle against any deep, whole-hearted conviction when it comes to doing what is necessary. After all, there was a United Nations Conference on the Human Environment in Stockholm in 1972, whose proceedings 'Sonny' Rhampal, former Commonwealth Secretary-General has described in his book *Our Country, The Planet: Forging a Partnership for Survival.*[7]

Of course world recession can scarcely have helped this time round, encouraging reassessment in favour of other priorities, as has been seen in a number of instances, including those that are not only immediate but also parochial. It seems evident that, for a time, 'the European dream' virtually collapsed, in domino style, this vision apparently having been regarded as an inappropriate and inessential luxury when backs were somewhat 'to the wall'. For the sake of us all, it must be hoped that any regression into old, outdated modes has been only temporary. With regard to tourism, continuing to operate as one for all their member countries in Europe are the European Union (and the EEC before it), through various channels, and the European Tourism Commission, this latter founded as long ago as 1948. Of more recent encouragement is that there was a European Year of Tourism in 1990.

To the green, in the sense of a gentle, non-intrusive, damaging or materialistic approach there is a 'bottom line', which Michael Ignatieff has delineated: 'We cannot simply be shamed out of the high-energy industrial life-style.'[8]

We are asking a lot if we require, as do authors Wood and House, that 'As well as the environmental issues, good tourists will be concerned for the economic, social and cultural well-being of the country they are visiting.'[9] There seems to be a problem finding out and fixing exactly what 'green' means in tourism terms; whether it represents a holistic approach to any tourism situation, whether it means rural tourism, tourism that does not harm nature, or whether it means developing community-involved attractions, for example eco-museums (see also Chapter 2.2). The definition of the Countryside Commission for England's Senior Countryside Officer, Peter Ashcroft, is of green tourism as a 'concept . . . developed in order to show a vision of how tourism can be a positive and welcome feature in the countryside avoiding the pitfalls of Mass Tourism and relating well to the rural scene'.[10] Ashcroft continues by detailing green tourism's features as he sees them. Green tourism, he says:

Is small scale
Is socially and environmentally considerate
Draws on the character of the countryside, its beauty, culture, history, wildlife
Works through local control, supporting the local economy and employing local people
Is value conscious and cares about quality
Brings conservation and recreation benefits.
Re-uses existing buildings and derelict land
Favours public transport.[11]

This appears to be in essence a 'small is beautiful' credo, and as such may be entirely appropriate and achievable in some instances. If small is beautiful, though, what surely needs to be addressed in the context of the modern world, with its circumstance of mass tourism, is where do all the tourists go who are the overflow from the small, green, kraals? Can mass tourism be contained in 'existing buildings'?[12] If not, what are the remaining numbers of would-be tourists to do with their time and leisure in order to fulfill their desire for the same experience? What is the provision the tourism industry can make, suitably, to meet this demand? Ensuing chapters will consider such issues as these.

The 'traditional' and 'green' options are, of course, not without their applications. This book's whole premise, after all, is that, **on the basis of information about all the particular circumstances pertaining to a particular cultural tourism situation, a selection on the strategy for it should be made from a range of choices.**

Now there are many circumstances in society which have produced, or are producing, the situation of escalating cultural tourism whose need for urgent and fresh management this book seeks to address. Among them are: better, faster communications; more leisure; an increased expectation of, and need for, entertainment and stimulation; and an ever-widening belief in an equal right of access to the same information.

The vital issue is how to meet, excellently and appropriately, the practical challenge that acceptance of the concept that culture is *of* all of us and *for* all of us presents. As Michael Ignatieff has said, writing of the famous, then Minister of Culture in France, Jack Lang, who has demonstrated well, though controversially, his own awareness of the point: 'Culture . . . means everything which makes up a way of life.'[13]

Quality: the goal and guiding principle

In any cultural tourism situation, the guiding principle, whatever the type of strategy chosen as appropriate, is to aim for **quality as the goal: essentially, to aspire to the very best possible in all the circumstances.** With limited resources a solution may be ultra-simple but it need never, ever, be other than of the highest possible standard. We do not need to lower our sights. Whatever we choose to do should have integrity. Appropriateness is about what is best, right, in a particular situation. What would be an appropriate tourism strategy for the Louvre would not be appropriate for a small village museum in Polynesia. What would be suitable for Stonehenge would be unthinkable in regard to Easter Island's effigies. A plan which would work for Blenheim, home of the Marlboroughs, could not do so for Monticello, house of Thomas Jefferson. There may be several plan options suitable for a situation, representing different mixes and variations in the elements in a package, with any one strategy representing an appropriate choice.

In making an *on*-site provision for tourists at, for example, a World Heritage Site, it would probably be inappropriate to produce a situation such as Clive Aslet's projection – 'Forget archaeology. With mock Roman centurions and the occasional spaghetti house, Hadrian's Wall would no doubt make a highly profitable theme park, in the style of *Carry on Cleo*'[14] – which followed the autumn 1992 announcement of English Heritage's review of its responsibilities. Such a provision might well meet the need of some tourists and the presenter, but it would be very unlikely to be suitable to a site's needs.

How to proceed

The art of managing and conducting cultural tourism successfully is:

i)   to understand that cultural tourism does not operate in a vacuum;
ii)   to know that cultural tourism is a 'major player' in the contemporary world scene;
iii) to realize that the cultural tourism situation is one in which will be included involvement of any, or all, of politics, economics, culture and sociology;
iv)   to recognize that the situation that is to be managed is dynamic;
v)   to recognize that culture should not be exclusive; in some way or another it ought to be available to all;
vi)   to know and understand the three main needs, those of the visitor, the presenter and of the heritage item itself, and then to create ways to, as far as possible, meet them all simultaneously and appropriately.

Any decision about specifics such as 'how to cope with the pressure of tourists' feet on a much-visited piece of cultural fabric' needs to be made within the wider context such as is outlined above. **The overall situation should be characterized first and then an action plan for managing devised and followed.**

The big issues condition strategy which in turn determines what the appropriate course of action should be in an individual situation. Isolated decisions are like plugging one hole in a leaky vessel, while water seeps away elsewhere.

Cultural tourism in society

To look at cultural tourism in society, of course, is to come back to the macro level of global issues, of which cultural tourism is certainly now one. A common approach is needed as the existence of the various world organizations testifies. As has been indicated, within this, we need to look at the needs of the visitor, the presenter and the item of heritage. When we know what they are, we can seek to satisfy them in an appropriate manner.

A phenomenon, apparently particular of our times, which Gilbert Adair has highlighted in the title essay to his collection *The Post-Modernist Always Rings Twice*,[15] is that of our current strong disposition to be satisfied with a second-hand cultural experience. This is armchair travel.[16] As I shall suggest, the syndrome has considerable implications in regard to the appropriate management of cultural tourism. After all, there are few of us who are denied access to an armchair and sitting reading about, or looking at pictures of, a subject; and in doing this there is little harm we could do to that subject.

Another phenomenon is now emerging. Cultural tourism, by virtue of ascending to such a mighty position in society, is in many quarters of the world being foisted with agenda other than those of its own discipline. The importance of tourism to so many has been noticed. In Egypt, which in 1992 expected over 2 million visitors,[17] a 'campaign of terror',[18] set in motion with 'explosions at Karnak Temple',[19] has been begun by religious fundamentalists against tourists visiting sites along the Nile. Their chilling message was reportedly that 'The security of tourism is tied to our security in spreading the message of Islam.'[20] Already there has been death and injury.

As has been stressed already, we are searching for ways to manage suitably a new, dynamic and high-profile situation. It will not be easy to handle this effectively and appropriately. The process of learning will be continuous and so, by association, must be the processes of educating and training. The need to manage cultural tourism appropriately is right up in front of us now. We must positively look for a new way forward. The opportunity is marvellous, but the responsibility is terrific.

In Britain, a Task Force was requested in 1990 by the Secretary of State for Education to look into tourism and the environment. The resulting report outlined a number of 'Principles for Sustainable Tourism',[21] among them that

> Tourism should be recognised as a positive activity with the potential to benefit the community and the place as well as the visitor.

This defines the dream neatly. So, with this in mind, we will set out.

Issues and questions

* Cultural tourism in its size and context as a major world industry.
* The role of tourism for achieving political, economic and social objectives.
* That the user, presenter and item or site all have needs.
* The types of tourism, such as green and eco.
* How a suitable and balanced tourism situation can be achieved in different and disparate parts of the world.

a) Can tourism be democratic; and can the cultural heritage be accessible to all?
b) What major initiatives in global society have there been in recent years which affect tourism?
c) Why is tourism a growth industry?
d) Who are some of the 'players' and principals in tourism, and why?
e) What are some of the main matters for consideration in regard to tourism and its operation?

Further reading

Toffler, A., *Powershift: Knowledge, Wealth and Violence at the Edge of the 21st Century*, New York, Bantam, 1990.
Turner, L. and Ash, J., *The Golden Hordes: International Tourism and the Pleasure Periphery*, London, Constable, 1975.

Part 2
Components

2.1

The user

In an effort to conduct cultural tourism appropriately, we should set out by trying to understand what the users of a cultural item or site – the tourists – want from the experience. In expectation, or hope, of arriving at precisely what do they engage in cultural travel?

Why are there cultural tourists?

Perhaps the most basic and common error a presenter may make in his attempt to comprehend what a tourist wants is to focus on a tourist's chosen item of desire itself – the travel object or destination – rather than to look deeper into what exactly are the elements of its attraction and why they should entice a particular person or group. If the latter course is pursued, then not only does it become easier to cater to a *tourist* satisfactorily but it also becomes much more possible to provide an attraction for that person which can meet a range of other needs as well – those of presenters and sites, for example. Essentially, with appropriate information it may be possible to diversify to meet tourist needs just as satisfactorily, or even more satisfactorily than if they were the sole objective, yet allow other needs too to be met.

Tourists are humans, so it is at human behaviour that we need to look in enquiry. Why *should* a person want to travel and, moreover, for culture?

1 Escaping to otherness

The starting point is the assumption that, whether or not most men 'lead lives of quiet desperation',[1] the majority, at the very least, lead lives which are for the most part boring and dull. Few people, it is suggested, find that their every-day lives provide them with all the dimensions that they feel they need. Most of their waking hours, and more especially the lion's share of their 'discretionary time', are allocated to trying to make contact with, or put themselves in line for some **excitement and stimulation**. Conversely, those people who do have varied and exciting lives may yearn for periods of **peace and quiet**.

According to our personal predilections and preferences, we 'see' fulfilment in different items and access avenues. Whatever our particular goals and their means of possible achievement, in the process of pursuing them a situation is created for entrepreneurial activity. In viewing humanity in this, albeit somewhat simplistic, way, a scene is nevertheless produced; and the scene set is that for the provision of services or 'goods' by one, for consumption by another.

The tourism industry, of which, as has been said, cultural tourism forms a major part, is just one portion of this whole sector which sets out to service humanity's needs. It is, however, an extremely salient portion since, as the tourism body industry is quite open about, its occupation is dealing in our dreams. While it will, of course, serve practical surface needs, the tourist industry in catering to them will also be meeting desires which we hold deep within.

2 Stated against actual requirements

In relation to education and status the following example of somewhat concealed motivations can be provided. Ostensibly, we may want to travel, or visit a museum, for educational purposes. Such a reason would be what we have told friends, or someone whom we are seeking to impress, or a market researcher; it may even be what have told ourselves. The reality might be that we do not want to go at all, because we are not interested in the subject in question, or we may even fear that we are not 'up' to the subject. The reality could be that we would rather be at the cinema than on a cultural cruise, or on a course at a country house, or touring a 'worthy' museum's displays. The clever tourism operator will interpret correctly the real need and cater to it in a way which both suits himself and his cultural site.

3 A variety of tourists' needs in relation to any one site

The problem is that there is no such thing as the average tourist. Tourists can be, and have been,[2] categorized into various groups by their motivations for travel. In the context of cultural tourism, in particular, it is possible to identify various main types of need of a cultural site. But a site is a site and, with the best intentions in the world, it would be over-optimistic and quite impractical to expect any one individual site to meet all or even most of those needs. The immediate and obvious solution is niche marketing, focusing on just one audience; but even that one niche might be physically too much for a site. Alternatively a site might be perceived as being capable of only satisfying one need while it is regarded as being very desirable for any or all of a range of reasons (see Chapter 2.2) that it should meet some more. A difficulty in general is that 'the picture' of the tourism situation in our quickly changing world is forever altering, and therefore needs constant monitoring for pattern shifts. The tourist demography is itself always on the move.

Visitor groups

1 New tourists and new tourist countries

A characteristic of global society at the time of writing is that quite large parts of it seem to be moving about, but not by a long way acting in the traditional westernized tourism manner. Many people are, perforce, leading the life of a nomad because of a resource imbalance of some kind. Parts of Europe, for example, are experiencing a new type of tourist, one who is eager to visit but who does not have adequate resources for so doing.

Example: New to tourism at home, and social tourists abroad

Places such as Hungary, and more especially Budapest, are under pressure from both west and east while they struggle to establish themselves anew as part of the western world. New and enquiring tourists from the west require the upper-market facilities to which they are now thoroughly accustomed, while impoverished refugees from such countries as Romania can for the moment afford to pay little or nothing for facilities.

A 'stage up' from the latter group described above are those eastern Europeans, homing in on such places as Paris, who require affordable facilities different in type and scale from those traditionally extended to tourists. In the summer of 1992 the tourist authorities in Paris were reported to be responding very positively and instituting a number of helpful measures[3] for visitors from the east. This general market of tourists possessing scant resources, to which the title 'social tourism' has adhered, is potentially huge, and on a 'sell 'em cheap, pile 'em-high' philosophy has presenter potential, but for it to be served requires products dissimilar to those of old.

Meanwhile, of those in the former eastern bloc, in Hungary, for instance, the old socialist practice of trade union holiday homes, at such locations as tourist honeypot Lake Balaton, seems to be continuing for the moment at least, despite a changed political regime. A particular destination is the peninsula encompassing a National Park with the picturesque village of Tihany forming a major attraction.

2 Older and younger tourists

Older, First World tourists are another general group on the increase at the moment. These people are seen as naturally inclined to be cultural tourists: their requirements from cultural sites are likely to condition the touristic experiences that are made available.

At the opposite end of the market for culture is another major group, having perceptibly different requirements on the ground: the young, very often student, backpacker.

Between these will be a massive division, in terms of how to cater effectively to their cultural tourism needs. Characterizing that division is the way in which each takes in information. In simplistic terms, while the one will be more attuned to words, the other will be more 'at home' with images, with visual information. In the main, the older group will have little computer literacy whereas regular computer interaction will be the norm for the younger group.

Example: The teenage market

For anyone who is older than a teenager, and would like to communicate with the younger generation, required reading should be 16-year-old Emma Forrest's *Sunday Times* piece in praise of screen information, 'Reading books is not worth the effort'.[4] She says, 'Not reading is our way of alerting the intellectual establishment that we have moved on. "Unliteracy" is our unique contribution to modern culture.'

3 Altered attitudes

There is little doubt that visitor attitudes are changing. Nowadays, we like different attractions, and different styles of presentation from those of centuries, decades, or even a year or so ago.

Example 1: Animals

In the western world, as part of an increasing environmental awareness, the display of real animals, in zoos for instance, is less liked nowadays. In relation to the ancient practice in Turkey and Greece (now illegal) of performance by dancing bears, Balkan Holidays managing director told *The European*,[5] 'Some of our customers have been very upset by what they have seen. It is up to us to help put an end to this barbaric practice.' Rather than the traditional zoo, institutions like the Worldlife Centre at Leicester, opening in 1995, are to be preferred. This will have 'live satellite links to the Serengeti, the Amazon and a coral reef'. For their needs to be met and their views to be obtained, 'Visitors will complete multi-choice questionnaires for a smart card, which guides them to exhibits matching their interests.' Among the Worldlife Centre features will be 'A sensorium with virtual reality gloves and headsets [which] will simulate what a spider sees or allow the feedback of a mouse through the equivalent of electronic whiskers.'[6] In general it is apparent that old attractions representing displays that are static are not going to be 'enough' to keep on attracting visitors.

There are, of course, other ways in which the tourist at a site does not want to feel discomforted.

Example II: The quality of the environment

Research by the European Travel Commission indicates, *The European* reports, 'that the quality of the environment will become a determining factor in attracting tourists'.[7] Contrasts of wealth and poverty such as those characterizing many Latin American cities, among them the venue of the Earth Summit, Rio de Janeiro, are obvious candidates. The tourist, though perhaps not so naive as to expect to view a truly Blue, Straussian, Danube on a visit, is unlikely to be happy to see the ugly 'Brown Danube' now bordering Hungary and Czechoslovakia, a result of a hydro-electric scheme from which Hungary, anticipating the ecological damage to come, excused itself in 1989.

Example III: Certain environments and certain groups

Whereas some rural refugees must have difficulty comprehending and feeling easy in the environment of big cities, so certain people – visitors from early industrialized nations and certain ethnic groups, for example – may not feel comfortable going out into the countryside. The discomfort minority groups may have with the English countryside has been highlighted by Black Network Chairman, Julian Agyeman. He believes that minority groups in Britain avoid the 90 per cent of it that is countryside either because they consider rural areas to be backward places from which they have managed to escape, or because they lack the confidence to go into them, preferring to stay where they feel secure.[8]

Albeit dissuaded through different criteria, other groups may find gaining access to some cultural sites – town or country – difficult or even impossible. The needs of the disabled, and of other groups with special requirements, though becoming both better understood and catered for in many places, still demand more attention than those of the general category of tourist.

Principal needs

To review some of tourists' principal needs: we travel essentially for one or both of two reasons – because we are attracted to something, or because we want to escape from something.

1 Escapism

One of the most important attractions for a visitor to a cultural site is its differentness from daily life. In effect, this either means a characteristic of quaintness or futurist sci-fi, since reality for most inhabitants of the westernized world is living in an environment of a level of modernity roughly equating to that of room-set presentations of out-of-town retail furnishing outlets. As has been indicated above, it is debatable whether tourists from developing countries would much want to view primitive pastoral agricultural

19

presentations; these perhaps still being too close a memory even for nostalgia to have 'set in'. The appeal of attractions portraying old industrial life, for example, the UK's North of England Open Air Museum at Beamish or Wigan Pier, may be as much about obtaining status from demonstrating the way of life from which a person has managed to escape, to better themselves, as about celebrating, having pride in or gaining validation from a vanished way of life that is missed for being seen as better than that of the present. Status can come from each and either direction.

2 Status

As has already been suggested, one of the principal motivating forces for visiting cultural sites is status. This encourages both the need to go where everyone else has been, to 'keep up', and the need for those who perceive themselves as 'leaders' to go where the mass does not go and do what the mass does not do. The former syndrome leads to tourists 'having to' go to Venice, Paris, etc., to the traditional tourist honeypots, which become ever more such as increasing numbers of people travel. As Donald Horne says of obligatory venues, 'In Italy one *must* see Rome. In Rome one *must* see the Vatican. In the Vatican one *must* see the Sistine Chapel.'[9] Referring to Susan Sontag's remark that 'Travel becomes a strategy for accumulating photographs' (*On Photography*, 1977), Horne describes tourists waiting for a religious service to be over and who then 'make their distinctive act of worship at the altar. They photograph it.'[10] The buying of souvenirs is also very often about status, taking visible proof of having been to a place back to friends.

3 Religion and spirituality

The matter of status points to the complex variety of needs which there may be of one site. As an example of the range of visitor needs of a site, that of Stonehenge has been more documented than most.[11] Among needs of Stonehenge portrayed is its use by different religious groups which may, to a certain extent, be conflicting. In Egypt, congregating at sites such as the Pyramids at Giza and Luxor's Karnak Temple, New Agers are coming up against Islamic fundamentalists. It seems that visitors' spiritual needs of sites may turn out to be among the most dangerous.

A fundamental, and increasingly important reason for visiting one place rather than others, since it seems to require for its fulfilment qualities essentially only present in a **real site** rather than a replica or substitute, is that of seeking spiritual satisfaction and stimulation from a site.

4 Research and education

In a summary such as is given in this chapter, it would be impossible to consider in detail the various types of visitor needs for research, education and other similar purposes. They range, however, from the need for raw primary data by adult specialists and professionals to presentations on themes geared to particular student age and/or educational curriculum, together with a range of requirements by gender, ethnic and/or religious groups, etc., which they share with other visitors.

5 Specialness and exclusivity

As has already been indicated to a certain extent under the discussion of status above, much of the essence of travel is about having, or cultivating a perception in others that one is having a better experience than either they or you would have at home. Incentive travel has been found to motivate workforce staff more than money, but Angelo Carraro of incentive travel package operator Carefree Travel has stressed the importance of the memorability of the relevant trip. He says that 'it must combine activities that most tourists would never be able to organise by themselves – banquets, ballooning . . . trips to places that are off limits to most visitors'.[12]

6 Ease and comfort

The vehicle of travel is all part of the image of the travel experience. The airline of Slovenia, Adria, chose its new logo with care, selecting a quasi-Austro-Hungarian art nouveau motif, needing to present itself as, in the definition of *The Guardian*,[13] 'fully conversant with the nuances of the era of the lap-top computer and business class travel, a country in which Japanese businessmen can feel comfortable'.

7 Gratification: shopping and eating

With shopping and eating a well-attested high priority for so many tourists, it is likely that a considerable number would be more than happy to go direct to these activities, without pausing to view the cultural site itself. Of course, a token view of the site should be available, just so the visitor could boast that it had been seen. Most important is that the tourist should be made to feel quite comfortable about missing out the site from his itinerary, otherwise he will not have felt good overall about the visit and will not have regarded it as a personal success. It is noticeable at many cultural venues now that presenters, recognizing the major demand for these traditionally perceived side attractions, are scurrying to capitalize upon them. At the Guggenheim offshoot in downtown New York, understanding the market associated both with its immediate SoHo retail location, and of the affluent sectors of Manhattan in general, from which it must draw its main audience, the Museum has a shop up front on the street with the gallery behind. Attuning to the SoHo lifestyle, the opening hours are late three nights a week. Gratification can come from buying the 'been there' status object; never mind, necessarily, about seeing the exhibits. The Guggenheim follows a trail blazed by Thomas Hoving, who cleverly opened up the Metropolitan Museum to a clientele which did not customarily tour museums. He did it by providing the general pzazz, and sleek retail shop and food operations in particular, to pander to a taste which those on the Museum's doorstep had before found catered to in Bloomingdale's, Bendel's or Bonwit's rather than within a museum's portals. Interestingly, the chosen title for his memoir of his Metropolitan period is *Playing to the Gallery* (1993).[14]

At the extraordinarily popular National Railway Museum at York, visitors can now 'pause for refreshment in the Brief Encounter Restaurant'[15] right in the middle of the South Hall, and in summer there is even a barbeque outside. The retail operation linked to a cultural centre that, in characteristic Parisian manner, looks certain to set a whole new order in both scale and style for the general concept is that created at the Louvre site. Already a major world cultural centre, the Louvre has apparently been allocated the role of *the* world cultural centre, with all that designation is perceived to entail in the global society of the 1990s.

8 The democratization of cultural attractions

Example I: Birmingham

The City of Birmingham has apparently engaged in the exact obverse of niche marketing.[16] It has targeted its whole 'local' community with its new wide-ranging cultural – in the narrow sense of the word – product. It is assumed, however, that behind the decision to go for a broad market base lay the recognition that a mass market was needed to ensure occupation of the many new seats set up in the City to view culture, year round; and that political expedience demanded strong local support for the City's initiative in 'going' for culture in a major way. The ploy is clever, catering to a market which has been shown to be there for opening up by successes such as those of James Galway, Pavarotti's 'Nessun Dorma' and Nigel Kennedy. In effect, Birmingham's particular product is culture democratized.

Example II: The Pompidou Centre

The phenomenal success of the Pompidou Centre as an attraction to visitors, whatever might be the traditionalists' view of it (a notable critic has been the writer Jean Baudrillard), is because it is a concept designed for a market which was not being well or wholly served before. In inspiration following André Malraux's 'Maisons de la Culture' idea, the Pompidou Centre set the tone for the democratization of culture, such as that now being attempted at Birmingham. As one of its architects, Richard Rogers, has said (of the Pompidou Centre and his later, unchosen design for the National Gallery), 'we sought to create centres that could appeal to everyone: children, tourists, and locals, students and workers, users and passers by. We wanted to establish not remote museums but vibrant public meeting places.'[17] There is little doubt that the young love the Pompidou Centre, continuing to visit it in droves. As an example, on a Monday morning, immediately after the Christmas week-end, a large group was gathered around the entrance, eagerly awaiting the time of opening. By being open in the evening, too, the Pompidou Centre is easily available to most people as a cultural attraction like a cinema or theatre; this is quite unusual for museums. For its comparison with the 'people pulling power' of some other cultural sites, the Pompidou Centre, albeit two decades after it was built, is worth studying carefully for its lessons.

Example III: Crowd-pulling successfully

Pre-entertainment queues are scarcely likely to thrill visitors much. At the Pompidou Centre, however, there is plenty of street entertainment to amuse waiting visitors. Disney may just be able to get away with it through clever management and the possibility of Mickey 'coming on by', but more positive diversion from a long queue is the ideal. The Bronte Parsonage at Haworth is one of many sites around the world ill-equipped to cope with its burgeoning volume of visitors. The typical tourist experience in London has pinch and pressure points because of the times of the Changing of the Guard, respectively 11.00 am in Whitehall and 11.30 am at Buckingham Palace, causing massive tailbacks at busy periods. It has actually been suggested that the time of Changing the Guard at Horseguards be altered to the afternoon to spread the load somewhat and create a better quality day for the tourist.

9 Providing a substitute object of desire

A tourist may not actually *want* to visit a site. He may be doing so because he feels he should, or as Urry says, 'To be a tourist is one of the characteristics of the "modern" experience. Not to "go away" is like not possessing a car or a nice house.'[18] The tourist may be going to a site he does not want to see because he is accompanying someone who *does* want to see it, so for several reasons it might be a good idea to determine what would create a feeling of satisfaction with his visit, to offer an alternative experience to make him content or to divert him.

10 Adequate information

Example I: On a visit

One of our basic needs, whether as a tourist or in any other of life's roles, is for information, to enable us to do what we want to do. In any circumstance, we feel uncomfortable when we do not know what we need to know. As a visitor, we are in an unusual situation. We are not on home ground, so we want to know what the 'house rules' are before there is time to become uncomfortable about not knowing them. Often we go to the wrong place in the wrong way through simple ignorance rather than deliberately. How can we 'keep off the grass' or not walk along a ruined wall, if we do not know we should not? But, of course, we need to be directed in a way that does not create in us a reaction of antagonism (see Chapter 1.1). An 'expert' may not realize, or may forget, what the non-expert does not know. Visitors need to be communicated with in a language and style with which they are familiar. It should be mentioned particularly here that just about everybody who can see can understand pictograms.

Example II: Pre-visit

The need for adequate information is in place at the pre-decision stage of travel, as tour operators apparently well know. However, while addressing the 'selling of dreams' aspect superbly, they sometimes appear to give less attention to the balancing need in people for 'feet on the ground' type of information. In wanting to be thrilled, we also need to know that we will stay safe. The mass of videos of 'other' countries now available help reassure us, and maybe even serve as substitutes for travel altogether for those either unable to face or to afford the real thing.

11 Fear, trepidation and comfort

Time and again, in the range of tourism situations, we demonstrate an underlying fear of going somewhere new. We are attracted but we are fearful. Going to meet potential tourists on their own territory is a good device for presenters. An organization called Explore, selling holidays ostensibly for the fearless 'market', nevertheless puts on slide shows round Britain, thus penetrating more deeply its perceived market. Maybe it is not so much that this particular market is necessarily fearful, but more that this market segment of the population tends less than many others to reside 'in town'.

On the JAL flight from Japan to Britain the Japanese traveller has the opportunity to view a video to pre-brief himself about London: a picture is presented of a fearsome place compounded of trouble and second-hand bric-à-brac. Someone who did not know London would probably feel like running from it fast as soon as they landed. A Japanese from 'safe' Japan could easily perceive London as threatening. Visitors *to* Japan might feel extremely nervous on an outward flight about how they would cope in that country but, fortunately, with the exception of watching skiing by virtual reality, there is unlikely to be anything on screen to feed their fears. In *The European* in 1992[19] there was a report of something similar to the advice given to those London-bound from Japan: this was France's complaint that 'Tokyo's Office of Tourism describes a city [Paris] of roaming gypsy gangs, over-amorous Frenchmen, and hotel muggings.' The report in *The European* continued by providing the alarming information that 'The current bestseller at Tokyo publishing house Kasakura Shuppan is *Information on the Dangers at Tourist Sites – Volume 1: Europe.*'

12 Challenge and excitement

A cultural site may represent a physical challenge or risk to the visitor – to climb it, walk to the top of it, or whatever. If most visitors to the site share that need, and that site is a heavily visited one, it is likely to be in trouble from erosion.

13 Dependability and accessibility

A visitor will be annoyed if that which he has travelled to see is not available to him. The sensible presenter realizes this, and arranges for repairs to be done out of season when a site can be closed to the public. An alternative to this procedure that is becoming fashionable – though what the public makes of these presentations is to be wondered at – is for a replica facade to be put up by way of consolation. However, it is amazing the number of cultural attractions that still cannot be seen at the height of the visitor season because they are under repair. Before his resignation, the Chairman of the British Tourist Authority, complaining about the length of time some monuments were taken out of public view, said, 'Tourists are alienated by famous sights shrouded in scaffolding – they can't even take a souvenir photograph.'[20] This report in *The Sunday Times* described how repairs to London's Albert Memorial may, in its view, at the time of writing in 1992, go on until the millennium.

Idiosyncratic opening hours, notably of a lot of sites in Italy, are such that the needs of visitors are clearly not site presenters' priority, although the Minister of Culture is avowedly trying to effect change. In the spring of 1992, at the instigation of its Cultural Heritage Commission and the Fondazione Napoli 99, the City of Naples had an exceedingly successful 'Operazione Monumenti Porte Aperti' in which, essentially, the doors of hidden Naples were flung open in revelation for the first time for 30 years or so.[21] A contrast to the situation in Italy is the practice of the North of England Open Air Museum at Beamish: the visitor who arrives in winter, when some attractions are closed, is provided at once with a leaflet informing him which are open.

14 Presentational styles and standards

Some visitors become accustomed to, and learn to expect, certain presentational standards at sites and museums. For example, the visitor to Hungary from a western old industrial nation, well-honed by the glitz and dazzle of a capitalist and consumer society and well-accustomed to the now commonplace associated styles of heritage presentation, may find the general atmosphere of earnestness and application prevailing at cultural sites and museums, though having in some ways a refreshing astringency, a bit depressing. The drab 'uniforms' – for example, the dreary overalls worn by custodians at Budapest's otherwise excellent, albeit traditional, National Museum of Agriculture – could be seen as engendering for the visitor a rather depressingly utilitarian aura.

What has been the attraction to visitors of the sometimes exaggeratedly old-fashioned display at the Conservatoire National des Arts et Métiers in Paris, part of which is housed in the church and refectory of the St-Martin-des-Champs priory? Some people will have been drawn to this area of the museum through reading Umberto Eco, to see Foucault's pendulum, but perhaps it is the spookiness that appeals, the batlike old flying machines hanging darkly overhead in the Church, the zaniness of old cars lined up the nave, the whole aura of a cabinet of curiosities? Much of the museum, however, showed a visual tiredness uncharacteristic of a Paris location. The Museum is now undergoing major refurbishment, which can be seen in many ways as a good thing but should the Church's idiosyncratic aspect go unnurtured along with the general process of modernization it would be a pity.

15 Ghoulishness and voyeurism

Ghoulishness, as witness the sundry chambers of horrors, Dungeons at London and York and similar attractions, can be a reason for visiting a site. Now part of the Golden Gate National Recreation Area, Alcatraz, the old prison island off San Francisco, attracts 750,000 tourists a year, though very few of its buildings are accessible to the public at the moment. Determining the level of necessity and judging the appropriateness of meeting the baser needs of humanity is, of course, a matter of fine judgement for the presenter.

Summary of visitor needs

As has been portrayed above, the varied range of visitor needs of a cultural site include: status/validation, education/research/information, spiritual uplift, entertainment, stimulation/risk. As is exemplified by the Disney attractions *par excellence*, overall it is rarely other than good sense to develop and convey to the visitor to a site a general sense of pleasantness, comfort and safety. How to manage a cultural site to meet the requirements of selected markets needs to be decided on the basis of information. And it is necessary to keep watching and evaluating continuously. By carefully monitoring their market, staff at the Museum of London perceived recently a tendency towards xenophobia and so they are staging an exhibition demonstrating, as the head of the later London collection reportedly said, 'that there is no such thing as a real Londoner. Everybody is an immigrant.'[22]

The necessity for close and careful analysis of visitor needs must be stressed. Once those needs have been accurately determined (or as accurately as possible), the ways in which they can be met most satisfactorily and appropriately, for visitor, site and presenter, can be looked at. With inadequate or inaccurate information, the real possibility exists not merely for making the wrong decision, in itself nuisance enough, but for needlessly subjecting a site to visitor wear and tear.

Issues and questions

*   Tourists' needs in visiting sites.
*   Newly emerging tourist groups.

a)   What are some of the major groups and needs of tourists?
b)   What do *cultural* tourists in particular want from a visit to a site?
c)   Is it possible for any one cultural site or item to meet the full range of visitor needs?
d)   A visitor need being defined, how might this be translated into a presentation which is appropriate at a site?

Further reading

Pearce, P. L., *The Social Psychology of Tourist Behaviour*, Oxford, Pergamon Press, 1982.
Ryan, C., *Recreational Tourism: A Social Science Perspective*, London and New York, Routledge, 1991.

2.2

The presenter

In this chapter, the needs of presenters will be considered. As a preliminary to this, it will be necessary to identify who these people are and what they represent.

Who are the presenters?

The direct presenter of a cultural site will be the person or persons immediately involved in **making a cultural provision for the visitor**. The presenter in a wider sense is the community which is **serving as host to the visitor**, and in this chapter I shall consider the needs and aims of both these groups.

Type I

The needs of a site's presenter are most likely to be to use a site: to achieve **commercial success**; to fulfil an **education or information role**; for **philanthropic or social reasons**; or even merely for **reasons of status**. To do so, unless he can move on to another site without difficulty, he will wish his basic resource, the site, to be preserved or conserved, otherwise he will not continue to have the same 'product' for his purpose.

Type II

A wider community and/or its governors or political leaders may probably have reasons more diverse than those above to present a site to visitor view. **Economic reasons** may well be to the fore, but along with **generation or regeneration of income and employment**; **social purposes** generally with **conservation**; and **reasons of politics, religion or status** also.

It is easy to see immediately that within these reasons are many that are likely to come into conflict if present in the context of any one cultural site. Many amalgams and permutations of the basic aims will be found, so a potentially complex situation exists. As with visitors' needs, presenters' needs of a site may be many and various.

The circumstances

In the developed world, the general attitudinal direction during the 1980s appeared to be towards deregulation and privatization and away from the post-Second World War stance of public resource provision. In the context of presenting cultural heritage to the public, this had the result of encouraging the emergence of a heritage industry or business. While some of its priorities may have been abhorred by many, that the heritage industry encouraged more emphasis on identifying and meeting the needs of heritage of the public could only be regarded as good. The recent widespread recession enabled a necessary time for reflection and contemplation on what had been good, bad or somewhat indifferent, about cultural attractions as they changed and proliferated during the heritage industry's headiest days. Tourism, it appeared, along with heritage, was recognized as a passport to commercial, or other, success. But tourism too now seems to be being re-evaluated in some quarters, perhaps too negatively and to society's overall detriment. In the main, tourism *is* a success story, one of the few of the later twentieth century. Yet in the UK, and to a certain extent in the EU as a whole, for example, there seems to be a reluctance to get together to manage it suitably and successfully.

That what was appropriate or not for the 1980s needs rethinking or readjusting for the 1990s and into the next century is fairly obvious. Society has changed, is changing, fairly fundamentally. It seems set to continue changing and ever more quickly.

Types I and II together, and society at large

Presenters of culture range from supra-national groups to regions and cities down to an individual with a one-room museum or single-megalith field. Perhaps the message most strongly emerging for all of them, for all of humanity, is that in pursuit of aims and needs we can no longer afford to 'walk alone'. We must act in concert, adopting an integrated approach. Richard Rogers has articulated the view in this way: 'If we continue to consider only our individual needs, to be selfish, to specialize rather than try to understand the universal implication of what we do, or if we retreat into a nostalgic dream of a past that never existed, rather than making best use of the most brilliant modern minds and tools, then our future is bleak, to say the least.'[1]

Yet it appears some parts of the traditional heritage industry are trailing behind – perhaps a slight situation of last in, last out? The opinion of the Policy Studies Institute is that 'The 1990s already seem to have developed their own distinct identity as a less financially-orientated decade, with values and standards in marked contrast to the commercial excesses of the aggressive 1980s

– they are already being referred to as "the caring '90s". Yet in certain respects the reverse seems to be the case in the museums world.'[2]

A co-ordinated and interdisciplinary approach

It seems that some people engaged in the provision of the overall tourism product fail to notice either their involvement in a tourism service or their interrelatedness to other portions of the tourism industry. At EEC level and in relation to the new single market, MEP Edward McMillan Scott has identified 'policies affecting the tourist industry that could be better co-ordinated. They include taxation, transport, consumer legislation, employment laws, environment and competition policy.' He continued, 'And we should also work with the countries outside the EC to maximize the potential of our continent.'[3] Before he stepped down as Chairman of the British Tourist Authority, William Davis was similarly trying to demonstrate the breadth of endeavour that was gathered within the tourism net, saying, 'Tourism is made up of a wide range of different but interdependent activities and operations. These include accommodation, catering, transport, tourist attractions, information provision and all the other amenities and facilities designed to cater for the needs of visitors.'[4]

Types I and II: mixed feelings about cultural tourism

It is tourism's capacity to embrace so much, and so many disciplines, that gives the industry its power of attraction to leaders and policy makers around the globe. Its very capacity for success is why it can inspire so much fear in so many, and cultural tourism, by its subject matter, may inspire the deepest fear and suspicion. The greatest apprehension, perhaps understandably, is not experienced by politicians or businessmen and entrepreneurs so much as by heritage professionals and educationalists, and in insular, disadvantaged or rural communities.

Inner city artisan areas and country areas in which farming no longer provides the sole viable way of living are natural areas for government to consider as candidates to host tourism, whether at international, national, regional or local level.

Supra-national presentations, such as blockbuster exhibitions of artefacts from around the globe composed into a group by theme, will almost certainly require a certain accommodation of need between the various presenters in order to attain their common goal. Many will be wary of the whole idea of moving an actual artefact, because of the danger of damage during transmission. The Region Transmanche may be regarded in both France and England as a nice idea but, as a creation which crosses an ancient cultural divide, it may find its needs are not always in neat synchronization. Coming to an understanding may be required within a nation, between different ethnic groups, for example. New Zealanders, Maoris and the descendants of settlers, have reportedly reached such a situation, recognizing that each in the past 'took completely different ethical approaches to the management of land',[5] but apparently there is now, according to Sir Roy Redgrave, the leader of a Serenissima tour, ' "a new type of New Zealander" with a common identity but conscious of their two distinct heritages'.

Attention has been drawn by Barry Parker of the Canadian National Aboriginal Association to the information that indigenous peoples who are presenters may not present the 'different' aspects and attitudes which their viewing visitors have arrived to see. In their burgeoning prosperity through tourism, with acquisition of the attributes of progress having been the reason for their engagement in the activity, such presenters may no longer represent the exotically different attraction tourists require. In changing because of prosperity from tourism, indigenous peoples may lose visitors to attractions elsewhere which appear more unworldly and interesting. Whether or not it suits visitors' chosen role for them, the need of indigenous presenters may be for progress.[6]

A nation may wish to ensure that its cultural heritage overseas is suitably looked after and presented. In Japan the Japan Art Restoration Project was begun in 1991 with Cultural Affairs Agency guidance, 'with the support of the Japan Art Research Foundation, Tokyo University of Fine Arts and Music, Freer Art Gallery and Philip Morris Co., a U.S. company headquartered in New York'.[7] It could be imagined that, within this group of supporters, their joint endeavour would typically produce a range of needs.

It is well known that French politicians and mayors display a propensity for making personal, or party political statements through the built fabric of their town, city or other constituency, while simultaneously achieving improvements to the quality of life for residents and visitors. The competition is usually to the general good. Many provincial cities in France, as well as Paris itself, have developed excellent cultural facilities: among many are the Centre d'Art Plastique Contemporain Museum, combining the Arc en Rêve, housed in the superlatively converted Entrepôt Lainé warehouse in Bordeaux; Norman Foster's Carré d'Art in its newly refurbished piazza with the Roman Maison Carrée at Nîmes; the revamped Musée des Beaux Arts at Rouen; Montpellier's revitalized and restored old town; and the centres of Grenoble, Clermont-Ferrand and Lyons.

Example: Presenting Paris

In Paris itself, it is interesting to contrast the conventionally clichéd provision for visitors by the French Ministry of Tourism under the aegis of the Ministry of Culture, entitled 'Paristoric', with that across the City at the Pavillon de l'Arsenal, although it cannot be denied that the former has considerable charm, verve and spirit, and is uplifting.

The 'Paristoric' provision is essentially a big screen, multi-slide presentation, with loudspeaker voice-over in French augmented by translated explanations in English, German, Italian, Dutch, Spanish, and Japanese, via headsets. A select version of Paris' history is outlined lovingly, presenting the city as a lady.

The Pavillon de l'Arsenal is an ultra-sophisticated presentation, the 1986 brain-child of Jacques Chirac when Mayor of Paris, providing information in a range of forms on the urban planning and architecture of Paris. The permanent exhibition deploys a large model, using screens with push-button control by the visitor of slides of buildings for an area high-lit on the model. The temporary exhibition 'Paris Sonore' was a walk-around, minimalist display of a geographical and typological cross-section of the life of the City of Paris, using sound and visual images. Few of the images were figurative in nature. Slide and light exhibits were activated by a visitor's traverse, while state-of-the-art headsets transmitted accompanying sounds. The creators of the Pavillon de l'Arsenal, and its outside collaborators from the private sector, produced a display about Paris which, in its essentially abstract style, served to stimulate and release a visitor's spirit and imagination.

Other matters apart, a difference in type between the 'Paristoric' and Arsenal displays is that the former can cater for quite large visitor numbers at a sitting whereas at the temporary 'Paris Sonore', catering for large numbers would be difficult. Both 'Paristoric' and 'Paris Sonore', however, in their different way, allow the visitor to have a personalized experience.

Imaging

Example I: The city

Competition between cities is, of course, not confined to those within France. Across Europe, devices to achieve a high profile range from attracting a European City of Culture designation to staging the Olympics or deploying the talents of globally recognized architects for the creation of signature buildings or urban schemes. Glasgow, Lisbon and the smaller city of Antwerp all used their European City of Culture designation well, Dublin and Madrid less so. It remains to be seen how, or if, the needs of cities so designated will be met in the future. Barcelona and its mayor, for instance, used the Olympics to start a process of regeneration which is still continuing, with the restoration by Gae Aulenti of the Museum of Catalan Art on Montjuic Hill, among other projects.

Example II: Nation unto nation, with constituents

Needs in the newly unified Germany have required particularly adroit handling and consummation, for presenters' aims are not always as one. Parts of Dresden are being slowly and carefully restored to a pre-Second World War appearance. It was only just before reunification that funding, albeit inadequate, could be allocated to restoring the Palace of the Electors. Restoring a former royal building was scarcely a priority for a Communist government, and work could only actually get going when a Munich bank supported the project. The Frauenkirche is now the focus of Dresden restoration and, as the site manager says, 'This has just as much to do with German unification as improving people's material living standards.'[8]

Berlin, meanwhile, still seems to be trying to resolve the needs and requirements of its key centre of renewal, the Potsdamer Platz. Symbol of past glory, 'the busiest spot in Europe',[9] so much is asked of this site now. Corporations such as Daimler-Benz and Sony want a status position, whatever need it may be used to serve; Hitler's bunker is at its core; architects perceive it as a status location; and for Germany as a whole, Berlin is to be the official centre of the new country, with Potsdamer Platz for a heart. Museums in different parts of the City are in a confused state too. Historically each has adopted different styles of funding – state in East Berlin, free due to subsidies in West Berlin – but essentially both in their different ways were announcing their wish for culture to be easily available, not exclusive. Now there are charges all round.

With tourism's economic might, to keep the peace makes good commercial sense. War in a country may suddenly frustrate its tourism presenters' needs in an acute way, causing havoc to their strategies and plans because overseas visitors have stayed away from fear. It should not be overlooked that neighbouring countries, or those which tourist planes need to fly over to reach their destination, may endure a similar sudden disappearance of their chosen 'market'.

Developing countries the world over, searching for ways to earn more income, see tourism as an answer to that need. Environmentalists and conservationists, with a global perspective, may regret what they see as a further threat to yet another 'unspoiled' area or culture, but on the spot the requirement to increase income, from abroad, may be perceived as a need that is more pressing and immediate. Mexico's aim was to attract ten million visitors in 1994, twice the number of only six years earlier. The government of Mexico hopes that 'new tourist circuits, such as the "Mayan World" linking ruins in Yucatán, Belize and Guatemala'[10] can be developed.

It should be remembered that not every country in the world may feel it can afford the luxury of not engaging in tourism, even if tourism is seen as inappropriate on some grounds and by some people. Tourism may represent the best opportunity for improving local standards of living.

Creating a product to benefit presenters

Example I: A solution

To develop a themed tourist circuit or package over an area may not cause too many problems if that area is a small island with objectives or needs that dovetail without too much difficulty. The award-winning 'Story of Man' exhibit on the Isle of Man comprises twenty-seven sites; there is some variety, but it is under single control. Judges for the 'Museum of the Year' Award in Britain praised particularly, as *The Guardian* reported, the 'splendid example of an intelligent approach to museums and tourism which is not bedevilled by party politics. . . . All shades of opinion appeared to be totally committed and have had the good sense to make the necessary funds available to make it work. There is a moral here which many local authorities need to learn.'[11]

Example II: A problem

Across the sea, on the British mainland, Barrow-in-Furness is one among many such places looking to tourism as a means to create jobs, as old employment opportunities subside, and to regenerate a community and its economy generally. Developing a concept entitled 'Incredible Journey' may not be enough to meet their need, because what is special about that, distinguishing *that* journey from others elsewhere which may be incredible too? Here the need is for interrelatedness, in the sense of knowing what your competition is, not to mention relating a chosen product to the necessary associated infrastructure and being cognizant of, and responsive to, *its* particular needs.

Changing places

Example I: Venice

Circumstances have recently changed in Venice: there has been a drop in the finite number of tourists and also the type of visitor has changed. Essentially, the resort has gone more downmarket. Like other traditional tourist resorts, Venice is experiencing an influx of east Europeans with limited resources, and reportedly many tourists from other countries are now on discount packages. The consequence is that the needs of the traditional tourist presenters, restaurateurs and gondoliers, for example, are, *they* say, no longer being adequately met financially. The blame for the situation is placed at the door of local and central government.[12]

Example II: Benidorm

As Venice sinks, Benidorm is responding to what it perceives as a requirement to go upmarket, to keep its market share in competition with rivals Florida and the Caribbean. Essentially, Benidorm is going green – literally in terms of planting trees, but also by cleaning up beaches, introducing new noise zones and imposing building restrictions.[13]

Division of need

A traditional village clash of needs was reported in *The European* in relation to Lagrasse Abbey, a listed historic monument, in Lagrasse, south-west France. The Mayor 'wants to develop the site for tourist and cultural events to revitalise the village's economy', whereas monks of a religious order which is trying to buy it 'want to shut Lagrasse Abbey to the public under an agreement with the existing owners'.[14] Lagrasse is a 'village officially recognised as one of the 100 most beautiful in France' and the Mayor reportedly wants 'to acquire the abbey for the village's benefit'. Such a scene could be replicated in many a village of the affuent world: one in which the needs of, probably, new residents, seeking a peaceful and quiet haven, vie with those of, probably, long-time residents, who need to make a living on their doorstep.

Direct and indirect needs

The business needs of tourism may be direct or indirect. Whereas a tourist attraction can meet economic needs in a direct fashion, a tourist site can act as a bait for bringing business newcomers to a place. In its plan to invite Universal Studios to put an amusement park in an old industrial area, Osaka City hoped that new businessmen of a certain category would be drawn to the area. Essentially the need in this instance, apart from that of the immediate presenters to bring visitors to make their attraction pay, was for a presenter, in this instance Osaka City, to use the attraction to draw particular visitors to a place. As an official said, 'If the planned park has an amusement place like Universal Studios, which is equipped with many high-tech devices, it will lure high-tech related companies and people from in and outside of Japan.'[15]

Using concept or theme to meet a need

In getting Los Angeles off the ground, railroad chiefs, according to urban theory lecturer Mike Davis, devised 'citrus culture', which to them 'seemed an ideal development strategy: attracting thousands of affluent investors, raising land values, reinforcing the region's "Mediterranean" image, promoting tourism, stimulating town-building, and above all, dramatically raising the unit value of railroad shipments.'[16] At any large site, potential sources of income other than those of the site itself exist, through the provision of associated necessary facilities, food and accommodation, for example, and of course transport.

The need to achieve status and fame, or to raise the profile for business purposes

A presenter may wish to use a site to demonstrate his own philanthropy. This was a particularly popular activity in the later Victorian period, resulting in the establishment of many museums and collections, especially in the USA and the UK. Individual initiatives and projects to create collections and/or establish museums include the Frith in New York; the Dupont mega-collection at Winterthur, Pennsylvania; Henry Ford's Dearborn near Chicago; the Getty Museum in Malibu; the Burrell in Glasgow; the Sainsbury Centre at the University of East Anglia, Norwich; and a range of cultural facilities established by wealthy industrialist benefactors in northern England's industrial cities. Sponsorship, currently crucial to the cultural industry, is 'about' meeting needs not dissimilar to those of a Frith or Getty, but with the emphasis more on effecting immediate business spin-off rather than setting up a memorial. The Colosseum in Rome is to be the beneficiary of a grandiloquent gesture by the Banco di Roma which, over four years, will provide 40 million dollars to 'stop further decay'.[17]

The needs of information and scholarship

Most sites have to try to meet the needs of a variety of presenters. Sometimes needs are met almost serendipitously, as in the case of Athens. Here the initiative to alleviate acute traffic problems has meant that archaeologists' general needs to find out more about the City are being met by having a mass of major excavation opportunities presented to them (including below the Acropolis), because of the establishment of a metro system.

Contrasting needs in the community

In relation to underground work in the environs of a World Heritage Site, a clash of needs has been unearthed. The objects of contention are Combe Down's disused stone mines, which residents and conservationists 'want . . . to be turned into a heritage museum, tracing the history of Bath stone',[18] but which the City Council engineers think should be infilled. In England, publicity has been given to conservationists' complaints, backed by many planning officials, that historic towns and cities are being ruined by householders' DIY treatment of buildings. As has been indicated, special interest groups with concerns about cultural sites range widely from conservationists, heritage professionals, educationalists, religious factions and a neighbourhood's residents to those with more overt commercial needs such as hotel and shop keepers, the transport and food industry, and the farming fraternity and its representatives. Residents at Broadheath in Worcestershire came into conflict with the Elgar Foundation which wanted to add to 'the hollyhocks and roses cottage', Sir Edward Elgar's Birthplace, a visitor centre comprising 'an audio-visual theatre, library, shop, café and car park'.[19]

Specialist needs

Example I: The needs of archaeology

The Archaeological Resource Centre at York fulfils the dual needs of its presenter, the York Archaeological Trust. It serves as a resource to educate people about the archaeological process, much as the Pavillion de l'Arsenal 'speaks' for architecture and planning, and it also brings in much-needed income for further archaeological excavation of, and report on, the city of York.

In inviting visitors to an archaeological site, the probable needs of the archaeologist have been well defined in the Centre for Environmental Interpretation's 'Introduction' to its publication for English Heritage, *Vistors Welcome*:

> You may wish to . . . show people that what you are doing is in fact a fascinating activity . . . to provide valuable insights into the lives of your site's previous inhabitants. You may wish also to show them that you, as archaeologists, are more than willing to share your enthusiasm and contribute to the community's sense of heritage.

> If you are a recipient of central government or local authority funding or sponsorship, then you may also want to show policy makers, local councillors, local residents and sponsors that their financial support is in fact yielding good value for money, contributing not only to archaeology, but, through presentation, to recreation, tourism and education.[20]

A number of presenters' needs are described in just that small piece. The 'Introduction' continues in similar and useful vein, advising archaeologist presenters of their particular 'selling point':

> Your dig offers the opportunity to tell a realistic story – based on the reality and immediacy of discovering and unravelling the information held on or in the ground.[21]

These aims, in their general spirit, cover the likely needs of most heritage professionals, whether archaeologists, museum curators, teachers or interpreters. Essentially they need to inform and educate, to create understanding, and to demonstrate accountability and usefulness.

Example II: Specialist and general needs

It should be mentioned that in explaining a cultural site, the expert may impose his own informational style upon the visitor, failing to understand the latter's language and medium of communication. Without doing so deliberately, he will be meeting his needs and those of his peers rather than those of a general audience.

Example III: Needs for rural areas

Presenters' needs of rural tourism seem to have a special importance and desirability. In the main, rural communities who seek their livelihood from the countryside do not make an easy living, and many do not have access to modern resources readily available elsewhere. For various reasons, the general aim of central and local government in a range of countries, together with other agencies of assistance and development, is to help rural communities survive and stay put. Agriculture is no longer a prime industry, but the countryside is seen increasingly as a recreational facility, so it is immediately understandable that a range of presenters want to put rural tourism in motion in a variety of places.

In his book *Tourism in Europe*,[22] Rob Davidson draws attention to the differences of interpretation in Europe. He also makes a distinction between agri-tourism and farm tourism, which latter may merely be the use of ex-farmhouses for tourist accommodation. In terms of cultural presentations in the countryside, the two distinctive types might be regarded as **eco-museums** (the idea of a living museum of a community, the concept of Frenchman Georges Henri Rivière), and the less specific **farm tourism** which can be regarded here as a combined way of livelihood encompassing, in varying proportions, farming and accommodating tourists on the working farm. (As has already been indicated, rural tourism for the purposes of this book is regarded as tourism occurring in the countryside.)

The eco-museum idea was 'to present the traditional culture within the natural environment where it had flourished and developed'.[23] Essentially, the main need was to help the locals, perhaps most importantly by encouraging them to communicate with 'outsiders', their guests from elsewhere. Among the French examples are eco-museums themselves, and also rural and farm tourism initiatives, representing a range of responses in pursuit of that principal need. At the Mont Lozére éco-musée, a scattered museum, the intention stated at the main visitor centre is to bring *'un souffle de vie à la montagne moribonde'*. The need for **community revivification** is explicit.

Protecting the ecological heritage and achieving the necessary conditions to maintain the local population are other needs. Touring eco-museum exhibits, scattered semi-derelict hamlets, miles from a major road, it is easy to see how much the need of the 'presenters' – whether they recognize it or not – is for the prescribed injection of a breath of life. Formal exhibits may seem full of bathos, in their primitiveness displaying a community's introversion, further demonstrated by a morose, almost hostile, failure to acknowledge, let alone communicate in person with the visitor from outside. The need, if tourism is to be engaged in, is for presenters to be helped to communicate with their visitors, to overcome suspicion and unease, applying equally forcibly in Hawaii as in rural France.

Maybe tourism is being forced on such people as an expedient and they themselves don't really want it, but one could also say that perhaps they *need* it. The same difficulty, the wariness of outsiders, seems to exist whether the situation is of a fully fledged eco-museum like that at Mont Lozére or the blending of agriculture and hospitality to visitors at certain farmhouses. Related issues deal with permitting access over farmland for walking and other suitably green tourist pursuits, as in the case of the Causse Méjean, which runs a tourism co-operative association and for which area there is a museum. If farmers need to gain income and new ideas from tourists they also need, in their own interests, to communicate that they are not engaging in such activities grudgingly.

Knowing needs and knowing how to meet them

Example I: Needs in 'primitive' communities

In their arrogance, it would be easy for tourists to imagine in a patronizing First World way that people from less-developed areas are in a dilemma or are confused about their need for tourists in their engagements with them. Professor Dean MacCannell informs readers in his book *Empty Meeting Grounds: The Tourist Papers*, 'The conditions of the meeting of tourists and ex-primitives are such that one predictably finds hatred, sullen silence, freezing out. . . . The micro-sociology of the arrangement between tourists and ex-primitives reveals an interesting balancing mechanism. Even if the tourists bring greater wealth and worldly sophistication to the encounter, the ex-primitive brings more experience in dealing with tourists. Most tourists do not repeatedly return to a specific site; they go on to new experiences. But ex-primitives who have made a business of tourism deal with tourists on a daily basis and soon become expert on the full range of touristic appearances and behaviour.'[24]

Example II: Needs which use tourists to the extreme, and in inappropriate fashion

Probably the most potentially confrontational need of a presenter is when he wants to use the tourist to a cultural site as a tool to achieve a purpose, and regards the need as adequate to justify any means of use, even if violent or extreme. This might seem to be overstating the argument but circumstances increasingly seem to demonstrate the importance attached worldwide to tourism and therefore, as a consequence, to the usefulness of tourists as a means of directly or indirectly achieving those needs. Tourism is such a lucrative industry that it is becoming a bargaining counter as well as an end in itself. But, as Martin Woollacott predicted in 1993, 'This year . . . may come to be seen as the moment when the commercial, criminal and political culling of the tourist herd reached a level which in some areas may reverse the otherwise remorseless growth of tourism and, in others, change its nature.'[25]

The range of needs of the tourist

Assuredly, the cultural tourist is carrying a lot of peoples' needs on his back. It remains to be seen whether he bites back against the pressure of feeding those needs in all their variety and strength.

Issues and questions

* Range and diversity of presenters and needs.
* The potential for incompatibility/competition/divergence in some needs.
* Because of its success, the colonization of tourism by 'outsiders' for their objectives and purposes.

a) What are some of the principal needs of a site presenter who is directly involved?
b) What might be a community's needs of a site in its midst or environs?
c) Might needs of a directly involved site presenter and those of the community surrounding a site conflict, and if so, how?

Further reading

Centre for Environmental Interpretation, English Heritage, *Visitors Welcome*, London, HMSO, 1988.
Hethrington, A., Inskeep, E. and McIntyre, G., *Sustainable Tourism Development: Guide for Local Planners*, Madrid, WTO/UNEP, 1992.

2.3

The item

What is an item of heritage? In the context of tourism, what are the needs of an item of heritage, and how may these be achieved?

An item of heritage: either a cultural site or cultural items

To look first at the question of what constitutes an item of heritage, it could be defined, in the context of this book, as:

i)   a cultural site itself, whether single location or scattered, or
ii) a cultural object or objects, of one or many types, housed at a location or locations.

Cultural heritage and threats to it from tourism: the example of World Heritage and world heritage

1 Definitions

In its World Heritage Convention of 1972, UNESCO defined the cultural heritage as:

> monuments: architectural works, works of monumental sculpture and painting, elements or structures of an archaeological nature, inscriptions, cave dwellings and combinations of features, which are of outstanding universal value from the point of view of history, art or science.

> groups of buildings: groups or separate or connected buildings which, because of their architecture, their homogeneity or place in the landscape, are of outstanding universal value from the point of view of history, art or science.

> sites: works of man or the combined works of nature and of man, and areas including archaeological sites which are of outstanding universal value from the historical, aesthetic, ethnological or anthropological point of view.[1]

41

Though specifically defining World Heritage Sites, the First Division in UNESCO's view, such characterizations serve reasonably as a general definition of all cultural sites, albeit maybe of less high grade 'importance' to the world. Essentially, cultural sites, whether World Heritage Sites or world heritage sites, share the same common characteristics, their differences being merely those of **quality** as defined on a certain yardstick.

2 Threats

In the preliminary text to the 1972 Convention it was noted that 'The cultural and natural heritage are increasingly threatened with destruction not only by the traditional causes of decay, but also by changing social and economic conditions which aggravate the situation with even more formidable phenomena of damage or destruction.'[2]

Tourism and its related activities were presumably such 'phenomena of damage and destruction' as the UNESCO Conveners had in mind. Eight years later, in his Foreword to UNESCO's *A Legacy for All* publication, Amadou-Mahtar M'Bow stated in relation to world heritage that UNESCO's aim had been 'to preserve for the present and the future the monuments that bear witness to the creative genius of man . . . and . . . to make these treasures accessible to the widest possible public – both to peoples whose heritage they are . . . and to all other peoples who are beginning to discern in them the premises of a new found universality.'[3]

These were indeed fine aims in principle for UNESCO, but as we all know now, with the increase in tourism, if it was not already obvious in 1972 or 1980–2, if the 'widest possible public' actually had unconstrained access to any of the world's heritage sites, many could not stand the strain.

Cultural sites and tourism: needs and obligations, benefits and opportunities

What are the needs of cultural sites, then, if they are to stand up to the threat of over-enthusiastic tourism?

Conservation and preservation, because they are costly, and in a troubled world sometimes perceived as a luxury, need to have a level of public support. An item of heritage is likely to be in some kind of context, so for its maintenance that context will need to be supportive in nature. Tourism has the capacity to help in generating this situation.

Adrian Phillips, when Director of the Countryside Commission for England and Wales, noted:

> tourism provides conservation with economic justification;
> tourism is a means of building support for conservation;
> tourism can bring resources to conservation.[4]

Theo Burrell, National Park Officer at the Peak National Park in the UK, has said: 'Local people must be able to make a livelihood. Tourism is a better alternative than other forms of economic development, if it too depends on the protection of the landscape. . . . Over-restriction may turn a local population against a protected area. Over-development, on the other hand, may destroy its character. . . . Tourism can be a means of making a local population aware of its heritage. That heritage will be of considerable interest and value to the tourist. This in turn can lead to positive support for conservation.'[5]

In the Proceedings of the Third Global Congress of Heritage Interpretation International, Russell R. Currie and Turgat Var, both of the Department of Recreation, Parks and Tourism Sciences at Texas A & M University, opined: 'The equilibrium of conservation and recreation must . . . be assessed in order to maximize the benefits and minimize the detriments of tourism.'[6]

The type of approach which the views above represent was embodied in the remarks of the head of the UNESCO-established body PATRICOM, Abdel Kader Errahmani, and reported in an article in UNESCO's *Sources* in 1992 in which the tourism role of World Heritage Sites was considered. The objective of PATRICOM is study of the development of heritage sites. Mr Errahmani said: 'We need new ideas and concepts that reconcile tourism and conservation with the need for sustainable development; a development that protects biodiversity, cultural identities, and at the same time the livelihoods of local people.'[7]

What, therefore, does a cultural item need from tourism, and what does it need either not to have at all, or not to have too much of?

It is generally agreed that many cultural items cannot cope with too much **pressure of feet, breath or sweat**, or of **fumes from motor cars**, or of **toxic or corrosive substances** generally. They don't need them.

As has already been indicated, cultural items do need, however, *some* public attention if the circumstances are to be created in which they can be preserved and treasured.

Site presentation

Example I: Ironbridge Gorge

Ironbridge Gorge, the various sites of which comprise a World Heritage Site, is vaunted as 'the Birthplace of the Industrial Revolution'. Overall the Gorge, clearly hell on earth when it was a hive of industry, had, until 'rescued' to become a Museum, a quiet melancholic air of depression and decay. Focal point of Ironbridge Gorge, as the name suggests, is its cast iron bridge, the first of a kind. The bridge has been restored and is closed other than to foot traffic, which is itself a huge entity 'in season'. Keen observer of Ironbridge, Bob West, while allowing that the cast iron bridge 'stands as a monument to the emergent industrial bourgeoisie of the latter half of the eighteenth-century' continues, 'I will also say that it represents exploited labour, a shift in work patterns, discipline and time, and that it stands as a monument to manufacturing and commodity production. However, most of these meanings are not manifest in Ironbridge but remain latent and for the most part lost, in the technicist framework through which the bridge appears as *industrial archaeology*.'[8] West opines, 'surely part of the appeal of Ironbridge is that its industry is countryfied'. He then goes on to say, 'Tourists have been visiting the site for more than a century, and rural metaphor asserts that they come and go like the swifts and swallows that dart above their heads; just as seasonal, just as fleeting.' Of the town around West says, 'Just over ten years ago the overall feel of the place was one of dereliction but the museum has changed all that and not entirely for the better. Post office, greengrocers, butchers, chemists, and small supermarkets, all somehow still impoverished, barely hold sway against the craft shops, antique shops, and endless knick-knack emporiums that all sell the very same glitzy junk. Added to this cafés, "tea shoppes", and restaurants come and go like speculative butterflies, puffed up on the golden rays of summer when the visitors flit and cash registers chatter, only to spend the winter in fitful hibernation.'[9]

We can all think of sites which have been completely changed by tourism. But what is contained in that which West describes is something more than 'change'. We can debate whether change is a good thing, in general or for a specific site. However, there is something further that can occur, whether in the process of a site being served up and presented for visitors or for other reasons, and that is a loss of its integrity, its 'soul'. And perhaps this loss is more serious than material loss like erosion, or other damage that is physical in kind. It is not just a sense of a site having been altered but of having been neutered or having had a 'face' that is inappropriate applied to it.

Example II: UNESCO headquarters, Paris

The 'soul' can go out of a site even through negative action such as neglect, or the failure to be nurtured. Sadly, the UNESCO headquarters in Paris seems to come within this category. Clearly, the building and its environs represent a noble dream, an idea maybe stifled somewhat now, and almost certainly one which would nowadays take a different physical form. However, even purely as a historical 'document' of how such an idea would be articulated for its time, surely UNESCO's headquarters is worth keeping up in the manner those participants to its inception conceptualized. As a public relations exercise alone, and especially for an organization whose concerns are education, science and culture, and one of whose responsibilities is the World Heritage Site List, it would seem worthwhile for UNESCO to spruce up its flagship, both the fabric and the facilities, for visitors. The UNESCO complex is a superb and revealing cultural artefact and still needs to be presented as such.

Promoting and de-promoting sites

Example I: Public information

The List of UNESCO World Heritage Sites is now presented in the handy form of a leaflet[10] which includes a large map of the Sites. Can this leaflet be perceived by the tourist as offering information as to what are the top world sites? World Heritage Sites, in easily accessible portions of the world anyway, must through their designation be candidates for great tourist attention and visitation. However, many World Heritage Sites will have been visited, or over-visited, for years before the signing of the World Heritage Convention.

Example II: Site access and presentation, and visitor management

Some countries, for example Egypt and Italy, are 'old hands' at tourism. Traditionally too, though, Egypt and Italy get a lot wrong in terms of their cultural sites and their relation to visitors. In a swingeingly critical piece, 'Sights for Sour Eyes', Ed Vuillamy has described the dreadful situation that pertains at many of Italy's cultural hot-spots, reporting the short museum hours and unkempt buildings with which countless tourists are all too familiar. He comments, 'No one can come up with a solution to the problem of tourism as the great mass activity of the shrunken modern world. On one side of the debate is the democratic–political argument that favours maximum access to artistic treasures; on the other, the cultural–environmental argument (often called the snobbish one) that such unlimited access – and the greed that meets it – has destroyed places like Florence, and will fast destroy others too.'[11]

A World Heritage Site overwhelmed by visitors in high season is Mont St Michel in Brittany. The formula of a romantic-looking building, atop a hill, on an island, represents an understandably compelling attraction, but so minute a site as Mont St Michel, by its nature restricted, cannot hope, without benefit of the most imaginative, radical and wide-ranging management, to cater to two million visitors a year, without being sullied deeply.

Compare Mesa Verde and Chaco Canyon, both World Heritage Sites, and Bandelier National Monument. All are Native American Indian sites in the 'Four Corners' area in the south-west USA. Mesa Verde and Bandelier, as sites possessing dwellings set in precipitate cliffs, were clearly not originally designed with visitor attraction as a high priority. In contrast Chaco, much like Stonehenge, had a role of great ceremonial importance to a large area surrounding it, and so in its prime was a focus of attention and visits. Now tourists want to see round them all. As a site Mesa Verde demands a visitor approach which should involve searching through scrub and trees before parting branches to spot, across ravines, rows of dwellings secreted just below cliff-tops. The reality is a nose-to-tail procession of recreation and other vehicles creeping along a tarred road in an appointed way, stopping at appointed places, with a firmly guided tour for pedestrians round a small selection of cliff-homes. It might as well be suburbia. Chaco, at the other extreme, can be a real adventure for the tourist if the time is right: access is by a long, ill-signed dirt road, in a landscape empty but for the occasional Indian roaming by on horseback or in an old car or truck. When the wide valley is entered there is plenty of room, and there are plenty of sites to choose from, but, above all, there is a huge sense of majesty, just as Chaco's creators intended its visitors should feel. To the casual visitor to Bandelier, the place is a Shangri-La valley, an impression which the short self-guided walk round the valley sites confirms. However, those with the time and temerity to go on a longer, self-guided trail will be in for a shock, since the highlands above and around are naturally harsh and inhospitable and little has been done to convey any other than that impression to the visitor. At Bandelier, both down in the valley and up above it, the **realities** of the site are communicated to the visitor.

Stonehenge, another World Heritage Site, would be fine if it were not for the visitors. Basically the monument is tough and if a sarsen falls it can, with sufficient effort, be put back up again. Stonehenge hasn't stayed 'sacrosanct' throughout its life, yet this doesn't seem to have spoilt it, or its appeal, overmuch. What is much more perishable is Stonehenge's associated landscape which, while it may be dull to the untrained eye, is a holy grail to specialists. This area is crossed by a main road which has the result of bringing masses of people deliberately (or not) 'right on by' Stonehenge. From sheer lack of anything better to look at or do in the middle of an 'empty' plain, people have tended to stop and want to look over the only obviously interesting feature in the landscape: Stonehenge. Managing these people while attempting to preserve Britain's main prehistoric monument and 'its' landscape is a perennial problem.

Enlarged roads necessitated by increased traffic, in the visitor season at least, can 'threaten' a historic site; but the site is often the object of the journey for which the roads are, in the main, required to start with. Such circular situations in relation to cultural sites – the object of desire under threat from **the very solution to accommodating its number of visitors** – are the very essence of so many a circumstance the world over in relation to sites and tourists. If the determination and resources are there, the site's needs can often be met in fulfilling other requirements as well. Along the Edward I 'castle corridor' in North Wales, a World Heritage Site, a motorway extension has been built to alleviate pressure of traffic. Despite the major works needed, the road crossing the river near Conway Castle has been put *under* the river, for environmental reasons and to retain the visual harmony of the site. The tourist trek to Cornwall through Devon, in a sense a *cul de sac*, is an associated instance of the seasonality of roads, alluded to above. For most of the year existing roads are adequate but in visitor season they are wholly inadequate, and so more and better roads are built across cultural landscapes to serve a spasmodic visitor need rather than a site's continuous year-round need.

Accommodating visitors and World Heritage

Example I: The Vézère Valley

Visual, and atmospheric, harmony have been upheld in France's Vézère Valley, whose decorated caves, among them the famed Lascaux and Les Eyzies, are a World Heritage Site. To have produced this situation in the Vézère valley, an area within a region, the Dordogne, that is heavily visited by tourists, is an achievement that is remarkable. It is worth, therefore, looking closer to try to see what are the elements of this successful story whereby the vital constituents of sites are protected while attaining reasonable visitor satisfaction.

In the Vézère Valley, farms, holiday homes, hotels and camp sites mingle in the essentially agricultural landscape, along with historic chateaux – the national historic monument of Chateau de Losse among them. There is also a range of historic monuments other than those of the prehistoric period (the actual monuments to attract the World Heritage designation), the Romanesque church in the pretty visitor-attraction village of St Léon sur Vézère, for example. **Principal roads are adequate without being intrusive** in the landscape; they often now divert round the valley's villages; numbers of **side roads serving, as required, as alternative or 'escape' routes**, are useful features in terms of **providing visitor diversions and spreading the visitor load.** The bucolic scene is marred only by an occasional superfluity of signage.

There is good management in the Vézère valley. Until the 1970s the condition and survival of the Lascaux cave were being threatened by visitors' breath. Now visitors park in an idyllic woodland setting, go to see the **replica** Lascaux II, sited below ground, in **guided parties**, awaiting their **time-ticketed turn** spaced out among the trees. Only specialists are allowed to visit the original Lascaux cave nearby, for just an hour a day. Again, the only jarring note is the signs, which are out of character with the site.

Tickets also admit visitors to the Le Thot attraction on a valley hillside a few miles away. Indoors, prehistoric cave painting is explained to visitors, while outside is a low-key presentation of some present-day animals whose breeds equate as nearly as possible to those of the prehistoric period; there are entertaining replica prehistoric tableaux, most of them static but a few have small, but significant, mechanistic movements. An ideal **picnic location**, the spot is opened up sufficiently to enable the visitor to have a **superb panoramic view** over the, seemingly somnambulent, valley of the Vézère.

Further down-valley, near Les Eyzies, is a visitor attraction similar to Le Thot, called Prehistoparc. On a **self-guided walk** along a side valley floor, through woodland and clearings, and up the valley cliffside (importantly, in terms of the success of the presentation, alternating between patches of light and shade), the visitor is presented with life-size, natural woodland coloured, replica figures in scenes from Neanderthal and Cro Magnon life. The Prehistoparc, as the brochure says, 'is not only a site of recreation and excursion, but also a place of reflection and perhaps discovery, like a book read on a stroll'. It continues, 'The site offers the public a visual, concrete reconstruction of concepts evoked in museums. The human and animal figures on exhibit in this park were reconstituted on the basis of the most recent anthropological research based on bony remains.'

The Vézère valley seems, in the main, to have got it right in **serving site needs** while offering **an appropriate experience for the visitor**. Perhaps one of the 'secrets' is that even though replicas rather than the real thing are made available in a number of instances, care is taken to present them in as suitably 'authentic' an environment as possible. Visitors to the valley sites *are* managed, but so subtly that they probably do not notice and feel that they are moving about entirely at their own pace and whim.

Example II: Versailles

With a big site, an option is not to marshal visitors too closely along set routes. Not telling a large number of visitors how to experience a site could seem a recipe for disaster in terms of protecting it, but might conversely help to the extent of spreading the load on a site relatively thinly rather than concentrating it. The World Heritage Site of Versailles, by its very magnitude – for Versailles was *designed* to accommodate a lot of people – and the indecision of visitors about which of the many available things to do, to an extent absorbs visitors, and any harm that they may effect is at least not too obvious. Visitors tend to span out over the site. A **well-concealed 'train'** travels along side routes, transporting visitors who do not wish to make the long walk, **past key locations**, like the Apollo Basin, to far-flung strong attractions, like the Grand and Petit Trianons. It would be simplistic to suggest that Versailles is not victim to visitors, or that there are not points of visitor concentration, pinch-points, in certain places at the site. But, allied to the continual work of repair and maintenance, Versailles' widespread capacity for accommodation is certainly a help in the effort of conserving the site in appropriate style. However many visitors there are to Versailles, the site always seems well able to dwarf them.

Example III: Small areas

Concentrated areas of attraction, historic towns or villages, or small historic quarters within towns, the fabric of accreted age and antiquity, can be very vulnerable to pressure. The atmosphere of such places, where there are no 'out of visitor hours', is, at worst, lost completely at the time when the site is swollen beyond reasonable capacity with hordes of visitors. **If the resident/visitor proportion is not maintained in reasonable balance, the very aura which the visitors have presumably come to experience will be changed.** For residents, even if benefiting from the tourist trade, the effects of such numbers must, in many other ways, be very deleterious to the quality of their lives. The site, meanwhile – a narrow medieval town or quarter, for example

– will not have been built to endure such an onslaught on its fabric. To all intents and purposes, neither the spirit nor the material of such places can withstand the influx of visitors that is imposed upon them. Examples, among many places around the globe, are: Sarlat in Perigord; St Paul de Vence in Provence; even the City of York. Conversely, a relatively **remote geographical location** as regards outsiders' access to it, and a relatively **low density home country population**, such as that which characterizes Bergen in Norway's Bryggen old mercantile area, can mean a site will not be under much threat from being over-visited.

The cultural object

Like a cultural site, a cultural object (for example an item housed in a museum, country house, or church) will 'demand' certain basics in regard to its role as a visitor attraction and a public source of information. Its instrinsic qualities will require certain appropriate types of treatment as regards **care and conservation**; and its type of material, its relative rarity in relation to other examples of the kind, will dictate other requirements. The object will have other needs such as where, why and how, if at all, it should be positioned in the public view. As with a cultural site, the cultural object's need will be to be in a situation, to have treatment, that is appropriate for it. As example, witness the special treatment given to the Leonardo cartoon in the new Sainsbury Wing of the National Gallery in London, designed by Robert Venturi: whatever the opinion of the Wing's architecture, few could deny that circumstances for the Cartoon *vis à vis* its public are now excellent.

Similarly, albeit in a very different situation – both because there is a range of types of objects to exhibit and due to the likely number of visitors and their interests – the display cases/racks in the basement of the Sainsbury Centre's Crescent Wing (which has been designed by Norman Foster) are superbly appropriate for their particular purpose.

The site: managing elements with verve and spirit

It is probably possible to be too purist about a site's needs. It seems all to the good and not inappropriate that visitors to the Pont du Gard near Nîmes, a magnificent Roman monument which is a World Heritage Site, can swim in the river that runs under it. Though the river banks may look a little like Riviera beaches at times, this historic site is being **enjoyed** by visitors, not merely revered, and a quiet arcadian grove is at hand for those who prefer to contemplate it more quietly.

The attraction of many countryside cultural sites is, of course, precisely their aura of isolation and contemplation, and in some instances their **instrinsic characteristics of danger** too. The easier the access to them, the more the site becomes threatened, both in its fabric and its atmosphere. Victim of its 'success' in England is the Pennine Way. How to achieve an appropriate balance will be considered in other chapters, but the Grandes Randonnées in France, long distance countryside footpaths such as those crossing through the Cévennes National Park, can be mentioned here as exemplifying the sort of best solution to be found. This Park is a member of the UNESCO Man and Biosphere [MAB] programme, which seeks to embody conservation and development within the management of 'natural resources' on a worldwide basis. For foot, bridle or other routes of transport to work, of course, the need is, as has been indicated above in reference to motor roads in North Wales and Cornwall, for their carrying capacity to be appropriate to their style and function. With footpaths in England (a small country), for example, as against many in France (quite a large country), the problem is simply that of insufficient space available in places that are appropriately accessible to the public for an adequate quota of paths to exist so that no pressure on any one of these is too much either for its fabric to bear or for its intrinsic nature to be spoiled. Many people walk a long distance path to 'get away from it all', to obtain spiritual restoration and uplift: were a route to be well populated, the essential 'experience' would be lessened or ruined. The fundamental difficulty is, of course, not confined merely to routes but to any sites which are victim to crowds inappropriate in size for the site's type and style.

How to meet the needs of cultural sites and objects appropriately

Various types of positive and negative activity can be determined in relation to the needs of cultural sites around the world.

The state of Italy's cultural sites has already been referred to, but it should never be forgotten how very many sites there are in Italy that require management. Urbino, painter Raphael's birthplace, is now without its city walls due to rain; the crisis at Pisa because of its long-time visitor attraction has become a cliché even though the tower has now been forced a little more upright; vandalism and atmospheric pollution at some sites in Rome mean the visitor sees only concrete replicas of sculptures, while the originals languish out of sight, in hiding.

The statue of Eros at Piccadilly Circus in London had to be repaired because someone swung on its arm. Vandalism, tourism and erosion seriously threaten the fabric of Easter Island's famous huge statues, the *moai*. Dubrovnik, a prime tourist venue and also a World Heritage Site, was made a victim by the war in former Yugoslavia. Flooding threatens to destroy a prime tourist site in Poland, the thousand-year-old Wieliczka salt mine, another World Heritage Site. Segovia, in Spain, is a city very dependent on tourism: its aqueduct, part of a World Heritage Site, has stone disease from industrial, vehicle and excremental pollution. The Roman amphitheatre at Sagunto, eroded by rainwater, has been repaired so over-enthusiastically that UNESCO's help has been invited to save it. Jerusalem's Dome of the Holy Rock, 'Islam's third holiest shrine',[12] is victim to status haggles between the monarchs of Saudi Arabia and Jordan over who should pay for its repair. The need for this was highlighted by UNESCO when it started an appeal in 1988, but the need is now more acute because of rain damage to the shrine. Water and tourists' feet are wearing away the many rock carvings from the Bronze Age in the Bohuslan area of Sweden. Not only have the Pyramids near Cairo been under threat from tourists climbing over their lower portions but, UNESCO reports, 'camels urinate on the limestone'.[13]

Even the ends of the earth are not able to escape. Visitors have penetrated Alaska, forging corridors of tourism which change old areas of wilderness and wildlife. Of such parts of Alaska, long-time resident Mesca Littlesky said, 'This isn't Alaska, this is how we present it for tourists, in comfort. Alaska isn't real comfortable.'[14] Meanwhile, it is reported that 'tourists are plodding a newly worn path to the North and South Poles – and posing one of the biggest pollution threats to the last unsullied continents of the world'.[15]

What do these few examples demonstrate about the types of needs of a cultural site and which need to be addressed? Clearly a site needs **to avoid pollution** as far as possible:

i) from human breath, human and animal excrement, vehicle exhaust fumes and harmful emanations from industrial processes;
ii) from weather and flooding; from misrepair, decay and long delay to necessary repair;
iii) from erosion, vandalism and misuse generally;
iv) from loss of integrity or ambience, from various sources;
v) from loss of its role as informational resource through destruction of its fabric;
vi) from inappropriate development;
vii) from mismanagement of various kinds.

No site is indestructible. All are finite resources needing conservation if they are not to be unacceptably altered through tourism or from any other use. More fundamentally, a site's very need, and justification for existence must be communicated effectively to the public, to secure that site's continued existence. A site needs **to educate about itself**.

Positive steps to meet the appropriate needs of a site

Example I: Depolluting and appropriate cleaning

The cleaning up of industrial and post-industrial sites is now widespread, both for general purposes of environmental improvement and with the particular intention of creating areas suitable for recreational purposes. An example is North West Water's scheme, whereby 'Local people and visitors alike will be able to enjoy water leisure activities', to clean up the UK's River Mersey.[16]

Example II: Developing environmental awareness in the tourism
industry

In Britain a Tourism for Tomorrow Awards scheme was initiated by the Tour
Operators Study Group [TOSG], and run in conjunction with the British
Tourist Authority and the television travel programme 'Wish You Were Here'.
(It then became the British Airways Tourism for Tomorrow Awards.)
The scheme encouraged the tourism industry to develop a 'responsibility
to contribute to . . . environmental awareness and . . . to ensure that there is
a proper balance between the demands of tourists and the need to provide a
proper environment for present and future generations.' (Information provided
by TOSG.)

Example III: Encouraging appropriate action and behaviour
by tourists

With the slogan 'Tourists Need Not Apply!', Earthwatch, the body 'matching
paying volunteers with scientists and archaeologists who need help on their
research and conservation projects', canvasses recruits to assist in 40 countries of the world.

Example IV: Managing people appropriately for a cultural site,
area or object

i)   Prague is a sudden new prime focus of visitor attention. As Vlasta
     Stepover, Minister of Tourism, has said, it 'is not built for mass tourism.
     . . . so the only practical step is to push people out of Prague'.[17]
ii) The National Trust for England and Wales is no longer advertising some
     of its most highly visited properties.
iii) At the Montaverde Cloud Forest National Park in Costa Rica, among
     several initiatives towards sustainable tourism, international hotel chains'
     efforts to come to the area are being fended off.[18]
iv) In the Austrian Alps, to combat too much traffic on the roads, electric
     vehicles now transport visiting hikers from point to point.
v)   In the Cleveland Hills in Yorkshire, an alternative route to the over-
     walked Lyke Wake Walk, the Esk Valley Walk, has been opened up.[19]

Example V: Managing to respect and meet the needs of a site's local
community

i)   At Ladakh in Tibet, with the added difficulty of a conflict over religion,
     there is the endeavour of managing tourism in such a way as to encourage
     the local culture to thrive while producing material prosperity locally.[20]
ii) At Taramundi in Spain, the inspiration of the tourism initiative is reviv-
     ifying the resident community and its way of life. As a local person
     described Taramundi's new, suitably small hotel, 'Twelve rooms have
     changed our lives. . . . But we have to be very careful.'[21]

Example VI: Achieving cultural interaction, social regeneration and education

i) In the depressed and multi-cultural Spitalfields and Whitechapel areas of London, the East End Tourism Trust, from its Brick Lane base, is using tourism as a vehicle for inner city regeneration and cultural harmony.

ii) In a large, post-industrial, working-class and immigrant area of the City of Paris the already widely popular la Villette Culture and Science Park has been established, with old cultural monuments as its foundation. In June 1992, a multi-variate, mass attraction entitled '*Contre la Marchandisation de la Culture*' was held there, a clarion call against cultural commodification.

In relation to cultural sites and tourism, initiatives such as those above show the need:

to **evaluate** a site and its needs, to understand its peculiarities;

to look at a site overall, in its **full context**, including its community and its economic and political background;

to plan for a site **long-term**;

to develop tourism concepts for a site that the site **can accommodate without unreasonable harm**;

to produce **alternatives** to inappropriate or over-use; even to de-market a site;

to **educate** about a site's needs, to encourage good visitor practice.

The range of site needs and the appropriate responses

Looking at cultural sites around the world reveals a variety of needs which are under threat of not being adequately met because of tourism. And this is without the problems of site management which would be presented if such plans came about as those reported of an owner of land through which Hadrian's Wall passes[22] – a World Heritage Site – wishing to sell off small portions of the site to tourists. Self-evidently, a site such as Modern Movement architect Erno Goldfinger's Hampstead home, newly acquired by the National Trust, will require different treatment from, say, the Great Pyramid at Giza, however alike both may be in terms of simplicity of shape and line. With cultural items, a Dégas pastel in a prime position in a much-visited gallery will differ in its care needs from what is required by one among a group of commonplace prehistoric stone implements in a remote museum.

The important thing is to assess what is appropriate for the particular site in visitor terms *having regard to all its circumstances*. And however much a site may be perceived as having relevance for future generations, should it not demonstrate *some* present function as well, for its existence to be justified may prove difficult.

The cultural site or object: a wider context

We are told that, 'principal trade associations now recognize that every landscape has its carrying capacity for tourism: demand may soar but there simply isn't scope for unlimited growth without courting the business disaster of environmental collapse.'[23] It is to be hoped this is so, but the need, professionally, to research, educate and inform about a site's needs is unabated, and is continuous.

In westernized society, in conservation circles in general, preservation of a site is assumed to mean preservation of the item itself. But in places where an acceptance of transience is part of the cultural ethic (Japan, for example, where encouragement comes through the religious beliefs traditional in that country), emphasis may be placed less upon the preservation of physical fabric, more on the maintenance of an idea. The Ise Shrine in Japan, which was originally constructed in the 8th century, is rebuilt every twenty years. Such a concept may perhaps have great value and relevance when considering how to conduct cultural tourism appropriately and it is an idea which will be discussed more fully in Chapters 3.2 and 4.1.

Issues and questions

* Showing *v* protecting.
* Long-term *v* short-term requirements.
* Concentration and overload.
* Caring, knowledge and expertise.

a) What are some of the tourism threats to cultural sites and items?
b) How should the demands of tourism and a cultural site or item be balanced?
c) What is the most appropriate approach to managing a cultural site for tourism purposes?

Further reading

Ashihara, Y., *Kakureta chisuio*, Tokyo, Chuokoron-sha, 1986, then published as *The Hidden Order: Tokyo through the Twentieth Century*, Tokyo and New York, Kodansha, 1989.
Cleere, H. (ed.), *Archaeological Heritage Management in the Modern World* in the *One World Archaeology* series, London, Unwin Hyman (now Routledge), 1989.

Part 3
Objectives

3.1 Attracting
Issues and questions
Further reading

3.2 Detracting
Issues and questions
Further reading

3.3 Educating and informing
Issues and questions
Further reading

3.4 Entertaining
Issues and questions
Further reading

3.5 Commercializing
Issues and questions
Further reading

3.1

Attracting

Parts 1 and 2 of this book attempted to introduce and define the principal and likely needs of cultural tourism. Part 3 will suggest, under the various chapter headings, practical ways and methods of meeting these needs appropriately and well.

This chapter looks at how to meet those needs when the purpose is to *attract* tourists to an item of culture.

The reasons for wishing to produce an attraction are most likely to be:

i) to make a cultural item attractive in itself, though perhaps only in order to produce revenue for its repair and upkeep;
ii) to create a focus of attraction by association with surrounding areas, which may have a greater semblance of attractiveness;
iii) to serve as a diversion from a visitor-overloaded item elsewhere.

Reasons why sites do not attract large numbers of visitors

In many 'old' countries, England among them, are numerous historic monuments – buildings, as well as items in museums – 'saved' at different times, with less stringent criteria of selection than nowadays. In our time they may pose problems of preservation in the face of low visitor numbers and interest, and of burgeoning maintenance costs. For every Stonehenge and Tower of London, there are a whole range of worthy but dull (and off-the-beaten track) megaliths and other prehistoric stones, together with sundry isolated minor castles, houses and homes, and out-of-the-way, small museum collections. They may have little obvious spirit or allure, or are simply in the wrong place to gain attention.

In the case of the UK, if Orkney's monuments were scattered along the M4 motorway corridor, they would probably be too attractive for their own good. Conversely, if Stratford upon Avon were to be relocated in Caithness, it would probably slumber almost totally undisturbed. It could be imagined that the worst problems experienced by the Peak National Park, in relation to numbers of visitors, would scarcely exist were it situated in a far-flung area of Lincolnshire rather than in central England, surrounded by conurbations. If the architecturally very appealing small towns of Whitehaven on the Cumbrian coast and Blandford Forum in Dorset changed places, their relative abilities to attract visitors would change also. Weobley or Ledbury in the County of Hereford and Worcester would probably be visited more if they changed places with Lavenham in Suffolk and Rye in East Sussex. (The latter are both also part of 'packs', the one Constable Country, the other England's Cinque Ports.)

Increasing and creating powers of attraction

The instrinsic merits of a cultural item do not alone determine its attractiveness. The item may have, or be imbued from outside with, a factor of 'value addedness'. That value may be spliced on to the item: it may be its manner of presentation, for example, or, if it is a moveable object such as a museum or gallery group, it could be the immediate context or setting in which an item is put. A historic canal which allows actual *use* as a recreational and leisure resource, rather than serving merely as a sight, has extra value, an attractiveness to a wider audience. It serves more visitor needs. Some way back from such immediate circumstances can be a situation of associated or add-on attractiveness, for example to be in close proximity to a good café or restaurant, to have nearby play facilities for young children, ramps for access for the disabled along with other facilities for people with special needs, plenty of seats, good car parking, etc., educational facilities, associated shopping opportunities and so on. Even less immediately, being on a good transport communication network, public and private, would bear greatly on an item's ability to attract visitors. In relation to associated resources, many Greek islands, for example, know what a difference an airport makes – whichever the need is, whether to attract tourists or not to attract them.

1 Distinctiveness

To be highly attractive in a competitive market, a cultural item has a strong 'head start' if it has something **distinctive** about it. The attraction of Aldeburgh, on the Suffolk coast, is its associations with Benjamin Britten, the Aldeburgh Festival and the restored Maltings concert hall at the river estuary village of Snape. Without the benefit of a **national venue** in its midst – the National Museum of Photography, Film and Television [NMPFT], housed in a post-war cinema building – Bradford would have been unlikely to command much visitor attention for its more esoterically interesting than prettily attractive 'Little Germany' cultural quarter. Even with this help, it seems somewhat of a struggle to get Little Germany in visitors' sights.

Items like a national museum represent a Unique Selling Proposition in the fight to bring in visitors. The Scottish cities of Glasgow and Edinburgh deployed many and various tactics to try to secure for themselves the new Museum of Scottish Modern Art. Halifax, a post-industrial city in northern England, not far from Bradford, should experience some regeneration to its local economy and its urban fabric though the attraction of Eureka! The Museum for Children, into its midst. On a site alongside the railway, approached by a yellow brick 'road', and with an inviting Discovery Road address, this attraction is essentially a private sector endeavour.

Dropping names

...m, bombed in the Second World War and with little or no historic ...l attractions (like many cities in Japan it has the disdavantage of not having any or many interesting old buildings left), is using a new gallery, the Kunsthal, designed by the avant-garde Rem Koolhaas, to attract visitors. The cachet in such instances is that the museums or galleries were designed and/or fitted out by **headline-getting architects and designers**. The Museum of Contemporary Art [MOCA] in Los Angeles, for instance, was designed by Arata Isozaki and is soon to be joined in its somewhat vulnerable downtown location by a nearby Disney Concert Hall to the design of Frank Geary. In 1996, a more overtly safe part of Los Angeles will be home to the new Getty Center by Richard Meier, renowned for his white buildings. Luxembourg ought to develop a higher visitor profile with its new National Gallery of Art by I. M. Pei, architect of the famous glass pyramid outside the Louvre Museum – provided, of course, the building gets built.

Star refurbishments create attractions too, as with the Museum of Catalan Art at Barcelona which is being restyled by Gae Aulenti who turned the interior of Paris' Gare d'Orsay into the hugely successful Musée d'Orsay. Stuttgart used the talents of the late James Stirling with Michael Wilford to put the town on the map with their Staatsgallerie. Stirling was also involved in the brand transmission vogue, started in Britain in the 1980s, with his restoration of warehouse space in the Grade One listed Albert Dock, to create the Tate of the North, a focal attraction for the post-industrial city of Liverpool. St Ives, a seaside resort also long popular as an artists' colony, is situated in deeply recession-hit Cornwall, a county that is now rather rejected and left behind as a tourist venue. But it has attracted a Tate and, moreover, one designed by 'name' architects. Interior designer Andrée Putman worked on the Entrepôt Lainé gallery in Bordeaux and helped to restore the existing Musée de Beaux Arts at Rouen. Norman Foster, together with Jean Nouvel and Philippe Starck, have enabled the formerly faded city of Nîmes to be firmly put back on the tourist map. Its Mayor, Jean Bousquet, hopes the Carré d'Art will provide a product with the same power of attraction in the south of France as the Pompidou Centre has in the north.[1]

Places such as these, whose essential pull is the artistic quality and calibre of their buildings, contents or style of display, will lure high culture tourists and addicts of design from far and wide.

3 Modernity

Despite its repugnance to some, modernity, in itself, is a stong attraction to many. Epcot, at Walt Disney World in Florida, was built on this premise. Poitiers, in France, is pinning its hopes on Futurascope, the theme park of '21st century buildings' 'where fantasy, dreams and advanced technology come together' to bring more visitors to its area. The success of the la Villette cité des Sciences et de l'Industrie, which opened in Paris in 1986 on an old abattoir site, has demonstrated how attractive an uncompromisingly high-tech, and educational, approach can be to a mass audience when effected with suitable authority, taste and verve. The young are accustomed to communication by chip and screen, almost to the point of disorientation seemingly (see Chapters 2.1 and 3.3).

The main attraction at Ipswich in Suffolk is no historic quarter, though these exist, but rather a listed building of the 1970s, the translucent Willis Faber office block designed by Norman Foster. Elderly visitors too can be attracted by modernity. On a visit to the 'Day at the Wells' presentation at Tunbridge Wells, it was entrancing to see the way in which a group of senior citizens who were only just capable of walking round excitedly donned headphones and enthusiastically toured the exhibit, accompanied by Beau Nash on tape.

4 Repositioned and presented

Tunbridge Wells is one of many towns and cities to have perceived tourism as a way of achieving economic and other regeneration. The historic Pantiles area had become distant and separate from the centre of the modern town and, until recently, had an air of run-down gentility. Now, with the 'Day at the Wells' as a **focal attraction**, and through the **restoration and improved presentation** of the historic buildings, the area has spawned speciality shops and restaurants to meet the needs of visitors and also provides a 'back water' amenity which is very attractive to local workers and townsfolk as well. Tunbridge Wells is similar to a lot of spa towns, cities and seaside resorts which at one time were much visited but have not managed to keep on drawing modern visitors into their midst without developing **new powers of attraction and altering and redirecting strategies to attract different market segments.**

5 Transport and communications

Changes in visitor type, taste and lifestyle are responsible for shifts in patterns of visiting. Changes in styles and concentrations of transport communications alter visiting habits too. Cultural attractions on completely redundant, or only partly functioning railway lines will have experienced a reduction in market share, unless they have developed alternatively good methods of mass visitor access. Similarly, for a new cultural attraction to succeed, to be a part of a good public transport communications network will be extremely advantageous in this respect. If communications to a cultural site are not good, then a way round the difficulty, such as **carefully calculated marketing and advertising**, perhaps **turning disadvantage to advantage** in some way – 'far from the madding crowd', 'way off the beaten track', 'an ideal area for hiking, bicycling', etc. – will be necessary. **Fewer visitors means more expenditure per head is required**, so a wealthy or high disposable income segment of the market needs to be enticed and catered to. And as has been proved for some time now, closed railway lines reopened as speciality railways can have considerable appeal to quite a broad market, provided, of course, visitor facilities such as adequate car or cycle parks are provided at line ends.

Islands which are, ostensibly, for obvious reasons, quite off main communications routes can and do develop roles as main tourist attractions provided they make it easy and pleasant for visitors to make their links with main communications. Ferries or horse and cart rides can be made to be, and presented as, attractive and pleasant features of visits, with the very difficulty of getting to a place being experienced as part of the fun. On holiday, with on the whole more time to spare, tourists may not mind a slow or complicated journey if it has compensating features such as a splendid view, great catering, or is inexpensive compared to other travel methods or other holiday activities. Often a journey is a cultural experience in its own right, for instance the Orient Express, the Settle–Carlisle line, the QEII, a MacBrayne ferry (the fleet which famously plys between the Scottish Highlands mainland and its neighbouring Islands), a canal long boat or a gondola.

6 Joining and linking

Theming and **packages** attached to already attractive destinations are useful marketing devices. In a sense, both London and Paris are doing this by developing attractions in areas needing regeneration but which are close to existing visitor sites in more prosperous sectors: Spitalfields, by the City of London, and at three of Paris' four corner edges, respectively la Villette, the Parc André Citroën on the old Citroën car factory site, and Bercy Village focused on an 18th-century wine store's cellar (with, just across the Seine, the Biblioteque Nationale).

The more visually unappealing, isolated or otherwise defective in terms of strength of visitor appeal a site is, the more it needs to be **marketed**, its **attractions promoted**, and **the way to reach it widely and well described**. National travel services, tourist information centres and other information points serve a useful function in this respect. But a welter of information, including probably that of a site's competitors, will be put before the potential visitor: in 'umbrella' information places such as this the style and method of display of a site's promotional material is most likely beyond a promoter's control. Specialist information centres, such as that on Paris' architecture at the Pavillon de l'Arsenal provided by the Mayor of Paris, or that which offers a distinctive multilingual general outline on film of Paris' history and heritage, 'Paristoric', in a relatively dull and under-visited area south-west of Montmartre, can introduce a place but they are no use to individual site promoters unless their particular site is included serendipitously. These sites are discussed further in other chapters.

Co-operative activity of various kinds between individuals or organizations with more to gain than lose by joining forces to promote a group of attractions, linked by geography or type, can be very helpful in the promotion of an individual site. This is more especially the case if resources are insufficient for each individual to 'go it alone' and do what is necessary in terms of promotion and marketing. Tourist boards serve as a 'halfway house' in this way, promoting an area in general along with the attractions of their individual members, and also offering seminars to members on a range of matters relating to tourism. Museums and other attractions can join forces with hotels or transport organizations to create special packages, like the Macclesfield Silk Museum joining with the Lukic-Belgrade Hotel nearby to promote 'Silk Discovery Weekends'. Such ideas are clever marketing. In producing ready organized packages, presenters are making it easy to go to their attractions, thereby adding value to the basic product which they offer.

7 Good information

Promotion through **signage and other information is obviously a valuable tool** for attracting visitors to a site, particularly when a standard style and format are used which are generally recognized as conveying a certain level of quality and type of attraction, like road signs giving directions to tourist sites across a nation. Sufficient information is most important in almost any situation, and should be of a kind appropriate to a site and its desired visitor categories. Suitably sympathetic, helpful and inviting information is likely to serve as a catalyst in a decision to go a site. Put simply, **you can't go somewhere if you don't know it exists.**

Good new signage has been a feature of the promotion of a new tourist area of the now very disadvantaged Rhondda valley in Wales, once a leading region for mining coal. The importance of seeing your information through outsiders' eyes (i.e. those of the potential visitor) is surely indicated by the example of Preston, the Lancashire city which in 1992 engaged in the banner promotion of itself as 'Guild City'. Without more explanation information like this is surely utterly opaque and without meaning or lure to a stranger to the town.

A summary

The characteristics of a decision to visit are varied. Some of the varied forces which motivate a decision to visit were described in Chapter 2.1. In this chapter, the starting point is to show how to use such needs to bring visitors to a site, directly or through using something nearby, or associated with the site in other ways.

Marketing

Essentially every site in the world is different. In theory, therefore, every site has a distinctive characteristic that could be used in marketing. Often, however, this characteristic is not distinctive or inviting enough to be used, at least on its own, to attract visitors in any number.

1 Remoteness

A remote location can be promoted as a retreat or destination for the connoisseur. To be a viable proposition for the promoter, however, the connoisseur needs to be so attracted by the place, or a particular characteristic of it, or its exclusivity, as not to care too much either about a possibly long or complicated journey to the site or about digging deeply into his pockets to reach his privileged location. Rwanda's 'monopoly on gorilla tourism'[2] meant that it could increase its tourist charges to a high level, thereby restricting visitor numbers and gaining more revenue for conservation. Attracting people to an accessible location should be quite easy, but perhaps lots of attractions in a small area offer the same type of experience? In this case the task is to encourage the visitor to believe that he has chosen the best from among several capable of meeting his needs, or the one that is distinctive.

2 Outreach

Outreach promotion has developed extra facets nowadays. To the traditional methods such as exhibitions, lectures and presentations, brochures, displays, promotional visits, etc. have been added computer simulations and home videos. Promoters thus have wider powers of attraction at their disposal.

A museum or gallery 'brand' can be used for outreach of a different kind. The spin-off Tates have already been mentioned. Another brand used to create an attraction in a new location is the Guggenheim: there is a Guggenheim in both uptown and downtown New York for a start (see also Chapter 2.1). The Victoria and Albert Museum in London has decided that a suitable location for its V & A Indian collection would be a derelict Bradford mill. As has been indicated, Getty is proliferating in various forms. The tried and tested marketing practice of **providing a new product under an established umbrella brand** so as to expand an audience without having to start from scratch to establish a 'name' that attracts is now being used in the culture industry as well. Leningrad's Hermitage Museum is establishing exhibition space in London, presumably as much to attract funding for the main location as to establish a voice to 'speak' in London about Russian culture.

3 Packaging and theming

Cultural attractions are nowadays promoted through a huge range of packages and under a mass of themes. The major theme in Great Britain in 1993 was Industrial Heritage Year. The series of industrial sites along Ironbridge Gorge have the designated overall title of Ironbridge Gorge Museum, as has been mentioned already. As has been indicated too is that among clusters created in France are working places of a range of types in a section of landscape which are linked together, under the title of eco-museum; they usually come with a visitor centre as main entry point.

Several post-industrial cities or regions of Britain have invited visitors to their cultural attractions through the media of Garden Festivals. Music and cultural festivals centred on particular places – Aldeburgh, Wexford, Edinburgh, Spoleto at Charleston, South Carolina, Salzburg, Aix, the Rio and Venice Carnivals – have burgeoned around the world. As has been mentioned, certain cities in Europe have benefited in recent years from their designation as a European City of Culture. Special events and living history presentations are other ways of increasing visitor numbers to a site. Developing an alluring add-on facility can enhance attractiveness, be it an adventure playground or *fête champêtre*, herb shop or cream tea. Indeed, the new introduction may be more enticing to some market sectors than the basic product.

4 By, or in, association

Association, with famous men or women, characters in novels, with culture, themes, etc., has resulted in visitors going to places that they might well not have ventured to for their instrinsic merits alone. Monticello in Virginia is the 18th-century home of a famous former President, Thomas Jefferson; it is a World Heritage Site; and 1993 was the 250th anniversary of Jefferson's birth, so in that year Monticello had an extra promotional handle to use to attract visitors. As is indicated by the example of Monticello, 'anniversaryism' is a way of bringing a site more to public attention. The method has become an especially popular promotional tool in recent years. And as an example of how to preserve integrity, to keep to a chosen dignified style and standard without gimmicks while winning a positive response from a mass market audience (not to mention handling a large visitor throughput of a small mansion with sophistication and grace), Monticello is a standard-bearer and hard to equal.

In the UK, among associations of this type are those with the Lake District. Wordsworth's golden daffodils lure visitors in spring, and all the year round the fact that this is the countryside of Beatrix Potter acts as a visitor magnet. In Yorkshire, David Hockney's illustration of the City Hall was used to illustrate the cover of Bradford's 1992 Travel Manual for coach and tour operators.[3]

It is doubtful whether the 'listed' but relatively ordinary Victorian school, or even the canal intersections nearby would attract the careful restoration that they are undergoing were they not in such close proximity to Birmingham's new International Convention Centre, National Indoor Arena and Symphony Hall. Here, a character environment is needed to help hold the attention of the captive audience, not to mention encouraging walkabouts in the new environs known as 'Brindleyplace'. Both Bradford and Birmingham are using culture as a promotional tool. In the case of Bradford there is a strong spice of Pakistani, Indian and African ethnicity. Birmingham, meanwhile, as has been indicated earlier, is extending itself across a whole wide range, 'pitching' with culture to gain wide mass market appeal locally as well as status in a European context.

5 Accentuating

While the ideal in developing an appealing attraction would be to reveal an entirely unique aspect of a place or item, accentuating and building upon a particular feature of a place's culture, past or present, can represent a reasonable option. It could be said that the more exotic a product's characteristic, the more will be its appeal. Novelty, 'otherness', as long as it is not offputting or frightening, is customarily quite attractive. Chinatowns are fun as long as they stop short of being so alien as to be scary, as are medinas. A range of ethnic quarters, 'old towns', even ghettos and barrios could be objects of curiosity and fascination for a short while if viewed from a position of reasonable safety, such as the seat of a big tour coach.

6 The alien or unusual

With power to attract because of its 'otherness', like a museum's collection of artefacts from other cultures and eras, is the timewarp place or group of objects or buildings. Calke Abbey in Derbyshire was judged worthy of care by the National Trust for its time capsule characteristic. In Spain the quiet, and so far untouristy El Rocio area, once owned by aristocrats and now including a designated National Park, the Coto Donana, has long been preserved by the Gonzalez Byass (sherry) family. Now opinions in Spain differ as to whether this protected area should be a 'green' tourist attraction or whether the ubiquitous golf course and hotel process should be applied on the Park's edge, threatening the protected area's very nature.[4] This case highlights how adopting a standard formula approach and ignoring or threatening the very distinctive quality of a place by proposing a tourism solution that is recognizably unsuitable for it is an inappropriate response.

7 Mass media

Television, films, fashion and advertising are now becoming recognized as powerful tools of promotion, to shift even – or perhaps especially – the 'difficult' product which may have no obvious appeal except perhaps a certain graphic quality. Being the location for a film or TV series can suddenly transform the local fortunes of towns, cities and villages, countryside or seaside, left out from the mainstream of modern prosperity. Backwaters are suddenly on the tourist map. In Britain, for example, the small West Yorkshire town of Holmfirth was inundated with visitors because it and its environs were the site where the 'Last of the Summer Wine' TV series was shot. Part of Provence, formerly not much frequented by tourists, is now thoroughly overburdened with them as a result of Peter Mayle's books and a TV series based on one of them. The run-down, art deco and 1950s South Beach area of Miami in the USA has become a trendsetters' hot-spot because, with its combination of rather outré picturesqueness and fairly dependably warm weather, it came to be seen as an obvious backdrop for fashion photography.

Around the world there are now over 200 film commissions. Somewhat late to the game, Britain is setting up regional film commissions: perhaps not surprisingly, in view of the relative poverty of its area in relation to other parts of England, the first to begin work has been the Northern Screen Commission. Further south, across the Pennine hills on Merseyside, Liverpool is developing a 'Hollywood on the Mersey' reputation.[5]

Potential problems and difficulties

Overcoming the in-built difficulties of a site or item, in terms of its ability to attract, will demand careful assessment and may require extremely skilful marketing.

1 Associated facilities

Eastern Europe needs revenue from tourism but so far lacks many of the necessary resources for customer care that present-day, western taste demands, such as high quality hotels, a decent standard of service, good roads and cars, and a generally pollution-free environment. Heritage items themselves may be in a bad state of repair and poorly managed by western standards. The

National Trust in Britain is being looked to as a model for providing appropriate heritage conservation and attractions.[6]

2 Suitable attractions for a market

Visitors from eastern Europe are coming to be regarded as a nuisance in certain parts of western Europe because of their numbers and lack of spending ability. Many have converged on Paris but here, as has been mentioned, they are in the main being treated sympathetically. Facilities are being developed to cater to the low financial resource level and needs of such visitors: this category of endeavour is being dubbed social tourism. It is reported that Père Lachaise cemetery is extremely popular with such visitors because it is a free attraction.[7]

3 Security and danger

Riots, robbery, muggings and terrorism are liable, for understandable reasons, to put off visitors. If the World Heritage Taj Mahal Site were in, for example, a part of the Middle East it is unlikely that it would attract as many visitors as it does to its location in India. As as been indicated earlier in this chapter, Los Angeles' downtown tourist district is a bit too close for comfort to the City's more dangerous areas. Marseilles is trying to make itself more attractive, attempting to get rid of its image as a gangster city: 'Tourists will be targeted by nationality, so the British will be lured by the fishing boat and terrace café charm of the Old Port, Germans by gastronomic delights . . . the Swiss by the promise of country walks and sailing, the Dutch by culture and history and the Belgians by the excitement of city life.'[8] The report continues: 'There will be a separate drive to attract business visitors, with the linchpin being a new conference centre.' The World Heritage Site city of Dubrovnik in former Yugoslavia is now desperately trying to recapture its tourist market after being a war-zone front line in 1992. Both its image as a tourist destination and a lot of the city's actual fabric need rebuilding. Many believe that this Croatian city was targeted by Serbia *just because* it was a tourist venue.

The presence of danger does not necessarily deter all visitors, of course. Indeed, their ability to instil a frisson of fear – the London Dungeon, for example – is the essence of some attractions' appeal. Belfast in Northern Ireland drew tourists to the Falls and Shankill Road war areas, as well as to the Sinn Fein shop and to the Linen Hall Library's Troubles Collection. Among the tourists to Belfast have been Catalonians, identifying with the Irish struggle.

Attractive qualities

1 The spectacular and fantastic

It might be wondered what was the attraction of the polyester Schloss, a replica of the castle of the Kings of Prussia, which initially was put up temporarily in Berlin during the summer of 1993 and which was an overnight hit with Berliners. Does its strong appeal rest in a need for fantasy and spectacle, for otherness (the original castle was replaced by a dour Palace of the Republic), for a deep-seated desire for a monarchy, or what? Perhaps Euro-Disney, interestingly now called Disneyland Paris, would have been more suitably sited near Berlin? Doubtless many a cultural tourism promoter would love to fathom the secret of the Schloss' success. Certainly it is a glistening spectacle for the visitor as he walks east down the Unten der Linden to Museum Island.

2 Inviting and exciting public meeting and leisure resources

Museums, collections of cultural items and information, have in recent years come under close scrutiny as to their position in the community and as cultural tourism attractions. They became part of the 1980s' drive to image cities, particularly those which were suffering from post-industrial decline and which possessed large populations needing new employment and economic opportunities and a viable contemporary role in society. As Deyan Sudjic has said, 'museums are urban pump primers. . . . The museum has become a central part of the way of life of the modern city, less a store house of scholarship and treasures than a place in which many of the conventional aspects of civic life can take place. By default they have become one of the few urban public spaces in which families and individuals can promenade and meet each other, a place to eat, to go shopping and browse in a bookshop.'[9]

3 Validation and reassurance

Museums have a range of powers of attraction. Analysing what needs a museum in a particular location should meet nowadays is a difficult and delicate task. The Director of the Museums of France, Jacques Sallois, pointed to the 'fantastic transformation of archaeological museums',[10] citing urbanization as a reason. Sallois said, 'Industrialization eradicated entire segments of economic and social activity. Everything possible must be done to repair that damage. Museums have a vocation to rescue that recent past. . . . Art museums, social science museums, archaeological museums and technological museums must all respond to the same types of cultural challenges. They are all in the service of the public or, more precisely, the publics.' At the WTO Seminar on 'New Forms of Demand, New Products', held in 1991, Neil Cossons, Director of London's Science Museum, predicted of museums that

'Their full range of roles would be better recognized ... and they would become a full and active partner in the cultural heritage and cultural tourism process.'[11]

In summary

What attracts a visitor to a place could be one of many things: a new display method; a new vehicle for traversing the site; a new level of ghoulishness in the exhibit; something like a conservatory in which visitors can sit, or a crèche, or facilities for other groups with special needs; the place may have been seen in the movies or on TV; it may offer a new long walk across previously in-accessible country; there could be distinctive food, good parking, special plants or animals; or it may possess the characteristic of producing a desirable amount of horror and fear in the onlooker.

Fundamentally, what a visitor seeks in an attraction is a quality of 'other-ness', of difference from that which constitutes his daily life. Either he will be looking for peace, quiet and safety, or excitement, thrills and sensation. Which of these he wants depends on whether the circumstances from which he comes are mundane, routine and dull, or action-packed, varied and nerve-racking. The escapee from stress and activity (unless a 'Type A' who apparently needs a permanent 'high', in which case he will want to keep up his sensa-tion level when on tour), will want to get away from it all, or perhaps regress to a childhood situation of simplicity. The person leading an uneventful and boring life may welcome quite a lot of holiday 'highs' in the form of risk, novelty and excitement. To provide for these basic needs is the aim of a presenter endeavouring to produce a suitable and successful attraction.

As has been indicated, an attraction needs to be appropriate to the place, its likely audiences and to the style of its promoter. Some of the most unsuc-cessful cultural ventures have been because the promoter was being either untrue to the place itself or to himself in his chosen style of product or promo-tion, and the public were able to see or sense this.

With, for example, the WTO predicting a 50 per cent increase in tourist visits to Europe over the next 15 years,[12] the tourism load will need to be spread more evenly if breakdown is not to occur at honeypot sites. This means that new attractions must be developed and, therefore, what appeals to tourists must be accurately identified in order for new locations to be a success. It has been suggested that France will contine to be Europe's leading destina-tion with Hungary, relatively, going into a decline. Yet Hungary has space aplenty for tourists and could benefit from this industry economically.

At the World Travel Forum in London, in 1992, it was said that it is expected that there will be more eastern European and Chinese tourists. If the right place for all these tourists is to be found, new attractions, that meet their particular needs, have to be produced. If the predicted tourism on-slaught is to be met in France, tourism will need to be more dispersed, both geographically and across the year. The president of the WTTC projected, at the 1992 World Travel Forum, 'With innovative thinking, we see good prospects for nature tourism in Africa and rural tourism in Europe, the latter as a long-term alternative to set-aside and stockpiling.'[13]

The general message seems to be to spread tourism to emptier parts of the world which, moreover, need it economically. In so doing, however, tourism presenters need to try to interpret accurately what needs are, not so much by having a surface look at the types of places that attract already as by identifying what those places represent in terms of their precise power of attraction. Another overtly altogether different place elsewhere can then be seen as possessing the same character of appeal as the existing crowd-puller, and therefore to have the potential to be a successful and appropriate tourism venue.

Issues and questions

*   Location and accessibility.
*   Communication and information.
*   Profile and distinctiveness.

a) What are some of the characteristics which distingush an attractive tourism site?
b) What might be the disadvantages in seeking to develop a new attraction, and how could they be minimized or avoided?
c) What are some of the ways of attracting tourists to a site?

Further reading

Centre for Environmental Interpretation for English Heritage, *Visitors Welcome*, London, HMSO, 1988.

3.2

Detracting

The use of the word 'detracting' as the title of this chapter is deploying it in the sense of being the opposite of 'attracting', used as the title of Chapter 3.1. Detracting can be approached negatively or positively.

The negative approach

1 Diverting

Perhaps the best, and probably the easiest way of detracting attention from a site is to use the method known to nearly every parent in the world and that is, simply, to present a diversionary attraction rather than saying 'don't'. Human nature is such that we tend to prefer to do what is forbidden: don't walk on the grass, keep on the path, etc. Doubtless more effective in keeping people where they should be is the request at Pecos American Indian site to 'Respect the rattlesnakes' right to privacy. Please stay on the trail.'

2 Replacement or silence

Encouraging a tourist to go to another site from one that is over-visited can take the form of producing a new cultural tourism product which is attractive and/or discouraging over-use of the first choice by reducing its actual or perceived availability. The first action requires positive marketing for something, the other requires demarketing of one sort or another. Lindisfarne Castle on Holy Island in Northumberland in the UK is over-visited, in part because of visitor concentration occasioned by access to the Island being restricted to low tide periods rather than its being available over a longer time as would be the case with most visitor attractions not regularly 'cut off' in such a way. A simple way to help discourage over-visiting of Lindisfarne Castle has been the decision of its present owners, the National Trust, not to advertise it.

Between Easter and the autumn, at least, London doesn't really have to try very hard to capture a tourist market. First, it is a western capital and most of these attract tourists. Second, it has good communications with the rest of Britain, with Europe, and by air from Heathrow and Gatwick with most of the rest of the world's main population centres. Third, it has retained since the Swinging Sixties era a worldwide reputation as a centre for shopping. If its cultural attractions were transplanted, say, to Dumfries in Scotland, or Port Moresby in Papua New Guinea, it is unlikely they would be visited anything like as often as they are in London.

3 Facility removal

Ways of detracting from a site, therefore, albeit somewhat negative ones, are:

i)   not to 'put about' its name in advertising or other material;
ii)   to sever or reduce its communications links;
iii)   to spread the word around that it is always crowded;
iv)   to remove a popular and/or useful add-on facility like a tea room, shop or car park.

The positive approach

The ways of demarketing a place are on the whole small in number and by their nature negative. A more positive way of distracting attention from a site, as has been indicated in general with the example of Pecos above, is to create, with diversionary purpose, an item of equal or greater appeal than the first, or an item that is different, all really to split a visitor group when it arrives on site, hopefully in favour of the new, more accommodating attraction.

1 Being realistic

It is probable that there will be a polarity of views about a decision on whether or not to try to reduce visitor numbers at a cultural tourism site. The difference of opinion is likely to be:

i)   between those people who regard present **economic benefits** achieved directly or via a site as the priority;
ii)   between those people who regard **conserving the site** as of prime importance.

The polarity is, essentially, between the **short-term and practical** and the **long-term and philosophical**. The decision, in its most extreme form, is between the relative importance of an immediate economic gain and conservation for future generations.

This chapter's purpose is to address the 'grey area' between these two extremes. This allows that: tourism exists; tourists want a cultural experience; it would be difficult to protect sites completely without totally denying visitor access; and in most instances to do this would be impracticable.

The general aim of this chapter, then, is to address the reduction, as far as possible in the prevailing circumstances, of the damaging effects on sites from tourism. The premise is that of trying to achieve a level of tourism that is appropriate to the site, to safeguard its future, but having regard too to its particular present-day circumstances which may pressingly demand its use as a resource for tourism. It is not the intention here to ignore what might well be the economic circumstances of a site, i.e. without its revenue, a community's position could be one of dire basic need.

If, then, it is generally accepted that a certain cultural site is over-visited, what are the methods that can be deployed to reduce its visitor numbers? As indicated in the opening paragraph of this chapter, looked at in its essence, what would appear to be required would be merely to put into reverse, to turn over, everything that was recommended in the previous chapter for attracting visitors. Looking at the situation less simplistically, however, and more positively, analysing the actual circumstance of 'detracting', or trying at the very least to make some visitors not visit a site when they would otherwise have done so, requires a more sensitive, detailed look at possible ways and methods to accomplish the aim.

2 Diminishing the effect of tourists on a site

This can be attained by:

i)   managing visits to a site;
ii) dispersing visitors over a wider area than the site under threat;
iii) diverting visitors from the site to another;
iv) developing a 'new' attraction;
v)   creating a man-made attraction;
vi) refusing admittance to visitors.

Clearly, the sixth solution is the 'best' in terms of site protection, but for any or all of a range of other reasons – economic, political, religious, social, cultural, etc. – this course may be impossible or inappropriate. If the sixth option is inadmissible, for whatever reason, positive action needs to focus around any or all of the other five, and maybe others as well. In all the five options, but especially those which seek to send visitors elsewhere, it is necessary, of course, to analyse exactly what it is about a site which makes it attractive. Is it location, price, its ease of access, its catering facilities or something else?

3 Identifying characteristics of appeal

In seeking to disperse visitors from one object of desire to an alternative, it is important to understand what appeal the diversionary attraction needs to possess in at least equal, better still greater, measure. Saying 'people like small historic towns' or 'families are attracted to country houses' is not enough: it is necessary to identify what it is about small historic towns that appeals. In the case of small historic towns, shopping in quaint, friendly, not overly busy and unthreatening surroundings may be the attraction rather than, *per se*, either historicity or that it is a town. The lure of country houses may be a house's sense of other-worldliness, that it 'brings back' memories from the past that are happy, that the teas are wonderful, that its add-on facilities provide something within the estate's boundary to satisfy tastes extending over a range of different age groups. As Hugh Pearman has written in this regard, 'Say what you like about the average, sanitized, over-restored, over-marketed, over-run National Trust property, or its independently run equivalent – such a place is a potent mix of culture and entertainment, providing virtually everything that the middle-class family might want in an afternoon out. . . . The children can play hide and seek in the gardens while the adults marvel at the Chinese wallpaper, and everybody can join up for tea and cakes.'[1]

Pearman remarks how difficult it would be to produce this sort of appeal at the 1959 office block by architect Erno Goldfinger located at the Elephant and Castle in London's inner city. In general, in Britain, modernist architecture has difficulty appealing to a mass audience; a pity, since it is often at places which could well accommodate, and would likely greatly welcome tourists and their revenue. As an object suitable for visitor attention, modernist 20th-century architecture is an obvious candidate but its lack of obvious cosiness seems to mitigate against its being adopted as a desirable venue by many visitors.

4 Limiting or avoiding damage

Managing a cultural property so as to minimize damage to it from tourism can be achieved in various ways, some obvious, some less so.

The visitor load can be spread by two simple expedients, if the site is suitable in terms of its character and size. **Several entry points** for visitors to walk through can be created, rather than just a single one, and providing **several small car parks** rather than one large one would also spread the load.

There have been many experiments with putting in paths of tougher, yet non-visually intrusive material in heavily trodden areas, for example those of England's Peak National Park, a popular destination for a day out with a large number of people. Here the existing fabric is being strengthened from beneath by a man-made fibre layer.

Boardwalks are a very useful device. Placed across fragile areas they allow visitor access without any or undue harm, at least from feet, though ecosystems may be unbalanced in other ways. Boardwalks also have the benefit of allowing visitors to penetrate regions that it would not be possible for them to reach by walking at ground level, due to the innate instability or inhospitability of the terrain or to the presence of dangerous wildlife.

On the Pennine Way, in the Peak National Park, it has been necessary to put down stone slabs to protect the landmass. Casting interesting light on the strong detrimental influence which can be exerted upon the fabric of a site via the popular media, the Park's information officer has described Wainwright, the writer of highly popular walking guides, as 'a major cause of erosion in the English hills'.[2]

Whether it be allowing access to a room of pictures, wall murals, furniture, delicate fabrics and drapes, or heritage swamps, woodlands and the like, it is inevitable that people will have some impact, probably deleterious, however carefully managed their visits are. **Limiting the hours of access** reduces damage, of course, but it does not remove it. It was suggested at one stage that access to Venice should be by entry-card. **Ticketing access, using pricing to spread loads, or to lighten them through sheer high prices** can help to a degree, though this last produces a situation of elitism.

Limiting the available types and methods of **transport** can discourage attendance at a site. On some islands, for example, road transport may be of a style to constrain visitor numbers. On the Danish island of Bornholm bicycle transport is the norm, as it is on Nantucket, off the coast of New England. Motor-bikes can cause damage over thinly soiled and other fragile areas such as grassland, not to mention the disturbance their loud noise can make to the tranquillity of a countryside location. Mountain bikes are also on their way to becoming a nuisance in that people are cycling across country not in the past regarded as likely, because it was not very accessible, to suffer detriment from visitor erosion.

Prepared and managed as a positive resource, however, cycle tracks are a most useful contrivance for developing diversions. They can link together disadvantaged and not immediately attractive places, which may still, through their ease of use and ready packaged character, represent an attraction to tourists. A long-distance cycle track placed and promoted well will help bring tourists to an area that needs them; by **not placing a track in an area that suffers a surfeit of tourists**, a discouragement is presented to visitors wishing to cycle while at that location. The longest cycle path in Britain, for example, skirts west of the heavily visited Lake District and through Whitehaven on the coast along an old railway track for ten miles. Should parts of a site in single ownership become worn, with good management, **routes can be realigned along different ways to spread wear and tear.** Where landownership of a site is complex, or where the site is confined in size, such variation may not be possible. Even if the former course is possible, there may be **pinch-points** that remain, like bridges, mountain passes or exits from a fixed point such as a railway station.

Cities usually have relatively more public areas than rural locations, but even though a town will have correspondingly more visitors than the countryside, it may actually be far easier to redirect or disperse 'ant-runs', using signage, than over private land in the countryside across which there may only be certain fixed rights of way. **Critical mass** is useful in this regard too. York is a UK City which attracts a mass of visitors but it now has so many cultural attractions for them to visit that some sites at least must not experience overload. The Louvre attracts a large number of visitors to its overall area, but a new dimension has been added to its complex, to all intents and purposes, with both the opening of the Richelieu Wing and, much more particularly, the completion of the Carrousel retail centre and excellently displayed excavated fortifications. All this allows for a far greater region of visitor dispersal. It would be surprising if some visitors, seeing queues for the Louvre Museum, or even before they got that close, did not divert to the Carrousel instead because they actually **prefer to shop and eat rather than regard art**. The Louvre's diversion has been cleverly conceived: since it is underground it has not been much seen in the making and a great deal of its impact has been hidden from view. Archaeological excavation as the work proceeded has meanwhile been carefully explained to people passing by the huge building site.

Subterranean attractions, or those set into the sides of hills, seem to be coming into vogue – and with good reason, since they make little or no intrusion on the landscape. In Japan, innovatory schemes include the Forest of Tombs Museum at Kumamoto and the set-into-a-slope Chikatsu–Asuka Historic Museum in Osaka Prefecture, both by architect Tadao Ando. In Ireland the Burren Visitor Centre is to occupy an old quarry.

An obvious way of diverting visitors from a cultural site is to place an **excitingly informative visitor centre,** complete with shopping, eating and lavatory facilities, on the route to the site itself. One of the less overt functions of the new visitor centre at the World Heritage Site of Stonehenge will be to act as a filter, encouraging a proportion of the potential visitors to Stonehenge to be 'drawn off' to a facility that meets their needs of Stonehenge satisfactorily without their actually visiting the site. It is likely that on a day of bad weather, at Culloden, the battle site in Scotland, the well-resourced visitor centre already serves this function. Extremes of weather, hot or cold, can make a visitor centre more inviting than an outdoor site, especially if the facilities giving information about the site are excellent. In arguments about whether and what type of visitor centre is appropriate to a particular site (such as the heated discussion relating to the Elgar Birthplace at Broadheath, in Hereford and Worcester), the ability of a good and appropriate visitor centre to siphon people away from vulnerable sites should not be overlooked.

A lack of suitable accommodation near or at a site will act as its own deterrent, confining visits to those by tourists living within a day's travelling distance or who have friends with whom they can stay nearby. Conversely, anyone wishing to develop a counter-attraction will get off to a good start if there is suitable – better still exceptional in some way – overnight accommodation near it.

As has already been indicated, the methods of transport to a popular site can greatly influence the amount of stress its fabric suffers. **Public transport** can be a great help in reducing damage. Rather than a mass of individual cars, existing railway lines – if closed they can be opened up again – can be the means of access for a lot of visitors, if an adequate train service is provided. Without cars but with trains, a site is at least not congested with a mass of vehicles, and it is less spoilt visually too, yet even visitors with special needs can have access. Railways, especially where the locomotive is steam powered, or if they pass through scenic landscapes, may be an attraction in their own right, but perhaps their most important role is conveying visitors, thus reducing the potential harm to a site from cars themselves or from providing car parking facilities. The Durango to Silverton railway line in Colorado offers the tourist an alternative to using a car along difficult, high mountain roads and, at the same time, helps reduce the visual intrusion of cars on the spectacular scenery.

Creating a diversion to another less-visited site can be achieved in a number of ways. As has been indicated, rendering the first site unpleasant in some way is an obvious, though negative method of approach. Sites which have always had, or develop, a problem in attracting tourists to their midst – Marseilles, certain parts of Italy, the former Yugoslavia, St Petersburg, parts of Egypt, for example – confirm that tourists can be put off if they feel they are likely to fall victim to criminal behaviour, terrorism, kidnap, war, disease, or just sheer harassment and pestering. In Corsica, bandits' thievery at *bureaux de change* has caused the closure of such facilities, due to their personnel's fear of attack or being taken hostage.

5 Influencing where tourists go

The pattern of tourism is actually far more subject to influence than is generally believed. Thus making one attraction better than another in some way that matters to the tourist market will probably lure a proportion of visitors to the former from the latter. Some countries are beginning to realize that, though part of their area may be overcrowded, other parts may be able to accommodate many more visitors quite happily; they are setting about making this happen. While Rome bulges with tourists, Ostia Antica, an ancient Roman-cum-20th-century Mussolinian city a short train journey away from the Italian capital, stretches out over a wide area and always seems to have lots of spare space which could happily accommodate more visitors than it does now. In Greece, for example, the visitor load is not spread throughout the country (or, for that matter, throughout the year): if tourists could be diverted to other parts of Greece, it would be better all round. With Greece's huge spread of islands, the connection between number of visits to proximity of transport is especially noticeable in that country.

Twinning a popular site with another that is little known will not, at least initially, make the latter more attractive than the former, but if the visitor finds the facilities at the attraction to which he has been encouraged to go more to his liking in some way, in time a shift in perception and attendance patterns may occur.

Getting visitors to a new attraction (and, by implication, away from another) can be encouraged in many different ways. Developing a quick, easy and inexpensive communications link to the attraction is an obvious incentive. Despite all Paris' other attractions, lots of visitors to the city now go to La Défense: since 1992, the Metro has gone right into the centre. Another, most important advantage in terms of its crowd-pulling ability is that it has an **eye-catcher**, the Grande Arche. Like the Arc de Triomphe, the Eiffel Tower and Sacré Coeur, the Grande Arche is highly visible from a considerable distance; as the visitor travels about Paris, it continually states its presence and presses its cause in the game of seeking attention.

To see the potential of a site which is not attractive in its current state requires vision. The start of making Miami South Beach a tourist destination (see also Chapter 3.1), once a section of it had been put on the National Register of Historic Places, was New Yorker Tony Goldman seeing the potential of the faded art deco buildings and buying them up. They were renovated and then, with the encouragement of publicity from fashion magazines, numerous spreads of which were photographed there – and thus the beautiful people were already there in number – other.trendsetters and finally the masses found it attractive.

As has been indicated in Chapter 3.1, serving as the location of a successful film or a popular TV series is very likely to boost a place as a tourist destination. It helps to develop a site as a new destination for visitors if it can be shown in all its glory or quirkiness on the **mass media**, for this will almost certainly create curiosity and interest about it. The next best thing is to develop an attraction with some association with a current fad. In 1993, dinosaurs were 'in' because of Steven Spielberg's film *Jurassic Park*. The sad tale was reported[3] of the small decaying town of Dinosaur, Colorado. It had tried to get back in the mainstream in the 1960s, in spite of its location on deserted Highway 40, by changing its name 'to benefit from traffic to the nearby Dinosaur National Monument'. Despite a distinct lack of attractions, it was hoping against hope for stardom in 1993.

To succeed, a diversion will need to serve any, some or all of the visitor needs outlined in Chapter 2.1 – and better than the object from which it seeks to divert visitor attention. A noticeable need is **to shop**. Probably not many people would have given much chance to Gateshead's Metro Centre being a success, before it opened, but it has been and has spawned quite a few similar such attractions elsewhere. Of course, shopping malls serve many more needs than simply that of a wish to shop. They are fantasylands. They are safe. Communications are good. Parking is easy. Entry is free. They protect from the weather; their 'climate' is always congenial. There is something for all the family to do. Highly importantly, 'presentations' are ever-changing: no museum could hope to compete with the mall in terms of the rapid change to its displays, and therefore with its ability to provide novelty attractions; the mall has the huge asset of being formed of a mass of shops each one of which will keep on producing an altering display. **To create a diversion from an over-visited cultural site,** then, the choice of building a **modern man-made provision** such as a shopping mall should not be overlooked. The ultimate manifestation of the shopping mall to date is the Mall of America, interestingly enough in Minnesota, hardly a number one visitor destination by other criteria.

In the autumn of 1992 Prince Sadruddin Aga Khan, Chairman of Alp Action, described the Alps as undergoing 'death by tourism'.[4] With reports that even such remote locations as Mount Everest (it is being inundated by trekkers' rubbish) and Antarctica ('pollution and aggravation of the wildlife')[5] are being damaged by tourism (although Antarctica is saved to a certain extent by its very short visitor season), it is clear that nowhere on earth is safe from being sullied.

The focus has been on the pressure from visitors at World Heritage Sites such as Hadrian's Wall and Stonehenge, and how and what the appropriate tourism provision should be. Newspaper comment on the latter has included the statement: 'It is now being belatedly acknowledged that, where remote and romantic places like Stonehenge are concerned, tourists should not merely not be encouraged, but actively deterred.'[6] Some among this pantheon of sites round the world (perhaps those in Australia where the concept of the World Heritage Site is regarded, and valued and treated seriously) may, by their high profile example, offer leads for more general application in the management and care of sites in regard to tourism.

It seems the view is starting to be held in some quarters that it is a myth to believe there is such a thing as sustainable tourism. The *raison d'être* of eco-tourism is that it tries to be an activity with low impact. It will, almost inevitably, though, have some impact. Eco-tourism has been criticized by Tourism Concern as being merely a tool for marketing. In this chapter so far, it has been attempted to suggest ways of directly or indirectly minimizing damage to sites by visitors. The most extreme option, however, is to generate an attitude in a potential visitor of **not wanting actually to visit a site** at all, thereby encouraging that site's preservation. As the quote above indicates, there are signs now that the pendulum is swinging this way. If we want to cultivate the attitude of mind of not needing to go to a site in person, what will be the alternative or form of compensation for the person concerned? The answer possibly lies in technological developments such as virtual reality [VR] and holograms, which provide an experience almost indistinguishable from reality. Removed or reduced from such an experience are the less pleasing elements of a site visit – the demands of energy, cost and time, for example. In this respect, the 'Rediscovering Pompeii' exhibition at the Accademia Italiana in London, in association with IBM, was extremely interesting. As the Institute's Director said in the exhibition brochure: 'Our aim is to show how culture and technology can be brought together to give you an opportunity to "rediscover" Pompeii for yourself. . . . Through especially created, interactive programs you can make your own journey into Pompeii.'

Maybe during our time, as designer Philippe Starck has already suggested, we will expect to make journeys via technology rather than in person. Alternatively, with a change in perception we might expect not to see the real thing in another way. With a change of perspective on the part of the tourist, and often landowner too, the Pennine Way, for example, might be viewed as a *concept*, rather than as a particular item or course on the ground. This would allow capacity for its alteration and renewal in terms of its actual physical representation on the ground, so we would not mind whether we saw, or were on, a cultural site that was actually that of old.

A problem to be considered in the development and experience of a site simulacrum is whether that dimension of spirituality so connected with actual physical attendance at a site can be or needs to be generated for a non-authentic off-site attraction. As has been said, however, this spiritual dimension is not necessarily even required or wanted by every tourist in a site experience. So as ways are sought for turning visitors away from old over-visited sites to new ones where they can be accommodated, considerable potential should exist for the type of method and approach outlined.

Issues and questions

* Substituting, fabricating and replicating.
* Diverting.
* Reducing access.
* Staying away.

a) Why might tourists not visit a site, and what might constitute a bad tourism experience?
b) What types of devices might be deployed to deter tourists from visiting a site, and why?
c) What might be beneficial about providing a diversionary attraction?

Further reading

Davidson, R., *Tourism in Europe*, London and Paris, Pitman, Longman and Techniplus, 1992.

3.3

Educating and informing

An appropriate educational experience is one that fulfils a teacher's need to impart knowledge to a student, and enables the student readily and agreeably to receive that information. In the context of a site, the equivalent would be an appropriate communications experience between a site's presenter and the visitor. The ideal is achieving a mutually beneficial dialogue.

Perhaps the most common error in communication is for the communicator to use his own natural or preferred style of communicating rather than that of the person to whom he wishes the information to be imparted. Museums used to be – some still are – particularly victim to this syndrome, their information adopting a lofty and dry 'know all' tone. This approach either fails to appreciate, or ignores the fact that visitors are unlikely to be able to share curators' specialist understanding and knowledge of a subject or even their general level of education, and that visitors' styles of communication might be different from their own.

1 Learning lessons

Example I: York Archaeological Trust

In terms of communication with visitors to a heritage site, probably the breakthrough was made by the York Archaeological Trust, with the Coppergate site at York. They regarded it as a duty and obligation to make suitable provision for visitors, treating them as both welcome and vital. From this experience, the York Archaeological Trust came to realize the methods that were necessary for communicating with the public of the present day. The Jorvik Viking Centre used methods more usually found in a fairground, amusement or theme park, and then opened its hands-on educational facility, the Archaeological Resource Centre, which now has an offshoot housed in the Eureka! Museum for Children at Halifax. The York Archaeological Trust has learned how to bring its subject alive for mass audiences, while maintaining its academic integrity.

Essentially what the 1980s heritage industry was 'about', in the UK as in other countries, was a mass of organizations learning the lesson that a huge audience could be reached with heritage information, provided that information was communicated effectively, i.e. in a way that was comprehensible to the visitor but enjoyable at the same time. The average education level of visitors was assessed and presentations were geared correspondingly. If a particular visitor niche was identified and deemed to be sufficiently large to be worth bothering with, or suitably necessary by other criteria, the attempt was made to produce information in a guise that was suitable to it.

Example II: The Eureka! Museum for Children

The Eureka! Museum for Children is representative of what was described above in that, ostensibly at least – and as a PR tool – children with parents, rather than parents with children, were identified as a market. As was indicated in Chapter 3.1, the main approach on foot to the museum is along a yellow brick 'road'. The museum's address is Discovery Road. Certainly (once the necessary entry fees have been paid!) a strong impression is communicated to adults that they are allowed in only on sufferance and that activities and presentations are geared to the very young. Essentially there are a lot of large and colourful visuals, many exhibits requiring active participation, a great deal of high-tech wizardry – children see how to send a fax – but also some core, old-time activities like shopping and visiting the bank. Staff, called 'enablers', are more like playgroup leaders; indeed, this new-breed Museum has been described as 'an educational playground.'[1]

2 Communicating information in visual form

It is not only children who respond to information transmitted visually. Across the world, many adults too are readily attuned to absorbing information in this manner. For a start, obviously the **illiterate** can be communicated with through illustrations, but so too can an **international** audience. This has been understood at a range of public facilities across the world, with their use of pictograms to convey information. Nations and societies whose written means of communication features pictures and signs may have a head start in the society of the future. The Japanese language, for instance, is not only visual, it is almost pictorial,[2] giving it a fluidity as a means of expression which seems to allow a degree of dynamism and freedom of expression which cultures with the written word as their main means of communication might envy. Regarding such languages as archaic could be a mistaken tendency; it seems possible that they are far better equipped for the coming world's future style and character of communication than those which deploy words. If we ever attain a common world language, it may be that it will be pictorial in style.

The world community is being encouraged to become more visually literate. We 'read' images on television, on videos. Our instructions to computers are produced through the building up of different combinations of signs, having a marked resemblance in this to the style of language of the Japanese, for example. With a lead in advanced electronics and technological innovation, its heritage of being first with computers, video games, VR, etc. plus its capacity for assimilating and using the best from other cultures, its language style, and an ability for changing old for new quickly and without regret, we should not wonder if Japan becomes *the* place of tomorrow.

3 Changing subjects and styles of communication

The subject to be communicated at or about a cultural site is as much liable to change and development as the method of communication; the topics and style of its system of educating will demonstrate a society's concerns. It might be imagined that it would always be appropriate that museums and cultural sites should shift the styles and emphases of their communications according to the context in which they and their material currently are. Since their purpose overall is conveying information about periods of time other than the present, however, that sites too are revealing, through their style and content, about the time when they were originally presented for the public, or were later refurbished or their collection regrouped, may be useful. For sites to be revamped or a collection to be re-ordered will not necessarily be for the best, educationally and for other purposes of information, if in the process one piece of information removes and replaces another.

Example 1: The Museum of African and Oceanic Arts, Paris

A museum and collection 'of its time' is the Museum of African and Oceanic Arts in Paris, housed in a building put up for the 1931 Colonial Exhibition. The place reeks of an era of unconscious European superiority in attitude to the rest of the world, and to dark-skinned natives in particular. It is an education in itself.

Similarly, fusty museums, with row upon row of the same type of exhibit placed on view, tell us about a time's style of presentation and approach to collection.

Certain subjects are only belatedly being addressed in museums, just as there are currently some things too sensitive to be acceptable for presentation as a site or in a museum – sites of recent riots in urban areas, perhaps? The USA is only now, on its home ground, facing up to the holocaust with the recent opening of the United States Holocaust Memorial Museum in Washington and its counterpart, although very different in style of presentation, the Museum of Tolerance in Los Angeles. A museum due to open in Bristol – a city with a history of profit from the slave trade – changed its projected name from the Museum of the British Empire to the British Empire and Commonwealth Museum, and is now destined to be called the Empire and Commonwealth Museum.[3]

Our culture in the western world is, outwardly at least, largely a pale **green colour** nowadays. It is also the style in this type of society to be well disposed towards **political correctness**. These tendencies show themselves in the methods and content of education, and find an echo in approaches to education and information at sites and museums. There is a predisposition to be as helpful and informative as possible, rather than to be secretive and unwelcoming. In the UK a Citizen's Charter has resulted in government commitments in print to offering improvements in services. In many places in the world recycled paper is much in evidence for leaflets and pamphlets. Issues relating to **minority groups** are being addressed; for example, serving one sector from among those having special needs will be the provision of braille information panels.

Among informational initiatives in the UK is the organization Common Ground which, through its Parish Maps Project, seeks 'to make people more aware of the textures, sights and experience of their local environments'.[4] Young people, in addition to using the traditional voluntary service routes, are participating in such schemes as the National Trust Acorn camps, undertaking physical work in the repair and conservation of National Trust properties. The nomenclature and imagery are, of course, significant implying, as does as a whole the Trust's acorn logo, growth through conservation into maturity. In an urban context, at Birmingham's Centenary Square, focus of its new cultural complex, citizens and visitors are being educated about the city's projected future role with an almost socialist state style sculpture, 'Forward', depicting the burghers bursting enthusiastically from the smoke stacks of old towards a new dawn.

The mission to inform, as seen at visitor centres in National Parks, State Parks, Country Parks, etc., has taken a new shape in the city, ubiquitous tourist information centres apart, with the setting up of generalized centres of information about the built environment. At the Pavillon de l'Arsenal, for example, information is provided about the city of Paris in the form of models, photographs, plans and special exhibitions, many using innovative display styles.

Most museums or sites have some sort of designated educational facility, which may be in the form of an education room, an education officer, special education and information packs, or material for various ages and types of visitor. Teachers are accustomed to leading, and students to joining in, study tours. Now most children are used to seeing enacted, or themselves acting in, **living history** at cultural sites, whether in the company of teacher or parent. The National Trust has established its own theatre company, which tours Trust sites. In 1992, the Counter Reformation was considered in the play *An Endless Maze*, whose aim was reported to be 'to examine motives, ideas and evidence rather than events in isolation'.[5]

Adult education was boosted in France in 1992 with the scheme of the minister then responsible for education and culture, Jack Lang. He introduced as a pilot scheme in Ardennes, Aquitaine, Calais, the Loire Valley, Provence, Rhône and Paris, a system for employers to provide culture vouchers, rather in the manner of luncheon vouchers. Among partipating venues were the Louvre and the World Heritage Sites of Versailles and Fontainebleau.[6]

Meanwhile various organizations – UNESCO, for example, through its activities and publications – continue long-established educational work; this apart from designating World Heritage Sites. Using a bilingual brochure on World Heritage, produced by Environment Canada and the Canadian National Parks Service, as a platform for educating and informing, Viviane Launay, Secretary General of the Canadian Commission for UNESCO, introduces it saying, 'Entrusted to our care, but not ours alone, for these sites are part of the common heritage of the human race and allow us as Canadians, to join the global family.'[7] The influential role of Canadians in expanding good tourism practice will be referred to in Chapter 4.1

4 Modern communication

Some of the traditional and commonplace types and styles of material giving information and educating people about cultural attractions have already been briefly described. Recently, however, there have been massive innovations in the method, type and style of information dissemination. We live in an information age. It seems appropriate in the context of the concerns of this chapter, and this book's subject, therefore, to take a deeper look at the newer, and most widely available methods of information communication. It is assumed that ways of communicating such as by exhibition or sign board, leaflet, lecture or book, are well known enough not to require further elucidation and expansion here.

In Chapter 4.1 reference will be made to Japan's computer generation, the so-called *otaku*. In our efforts to educate the next generation, it could be that we are in danger of not paying adequate attention to a large cultural division that has occurred in recent years: the divide occasioned by modern **technology**, and more especially the computer. On one side are those who cannot, or will not, use a computer; on the other are those for whom using a computer is an everyday occurrence. It is similar, but much, much, more prevalent, to the divide which earlier separated (and sometimes still does) those who do and do not watch television. In terms of education, these divides can be the result of a museum or cultural site presenter being out of touch, and failing to understand how best to communicate with his young audience.

An interesting article in this respect was published in UNESCO's *Museum* with the title 'For lots of us, museum rhymes with humdrum'.[8] Written by two children, Sandrine Rona–Beaulieu and Stéphane Janin, it was the result of a survey of adolescent children in a **multi-ethnic** class at a school in a Parisian artisan neighbourhood. It begins: 'A Museum usually means a compulsory class trip led by one of the teachers. Students can't ever choose the museum – that's always done by the teachers, who want to use the museum to liven up their lessons. The only problem is, teachers aren't necessarily capable of sparking the class' interest in the topic they have chosen.' The authors observe, 'Going to museums with your school doesn't make you want to go back on your own or with friends at the weekend. Young people prefer different kinds of amusement when they're free. . . . It's not the "in" thing to go to museums.' Of some museums' communications, they say, 'Museum guides from the old school – the ones who reel off a speech they've learned by heart – don't make us feel like going to museums to listen to them and their boring spiels don't inspire us to ask questions, discover new things.'

Of museums' efforts at publicizing themselves, these young writers complain, 'You never hear about museums in the street or on the Metro, or on the television or radio, whereas any newspaper will provide you with a complete list of films, plays and concerts. . . . Going to the cinema is an easy thing to do, while going to a museum is quite an exploit.' As to how museums should promote their facilities, Sandrine and Stéphane say, 'One idea would be to put up museum advertisements in the schools and change them periodically. Distributing pamphlets in classes is another, along with holding contests and showing commercials on prime-time television between spots for detergents and disposable nappies, advertising in magazines read by young people, in television guides, on independent radio stations.'

This article has been quoted extensively because it reveals a lot about the way the young feel they are (or rather, as they consider, are not) communicated with by teachers and museum officials. Rarely do television or radio get the credit they deserve for providing general information, let alone for their capacity for chance, serendipitous transmittal of new information to an audience. The 'random' element, the 'accident' is, of course, only in relation to the receiver: as far as a TV or radio station is concerned, it will have planned its schedules meticulously. The point has been encapsulated by Alan Bennett, when introducing his retrospective view of BBC television, 'A Night in with Alan Bennett', on 5 July 1992. He said: 'One of the virtues of television is that we are able to blunder into watching a programme we hadn't intended to watch. There is great virtue in the random. We don't always know what we want, where we are going. We are not the single-minded customer which cable TV is predicated on.'

The National Museum of Photography, Film and Television [NMPFT], located at Bradford, in the north of England, claims it 'is now the most popular national museum outside London'. If this is so, it is as well to ask why, and especially since many might regard its location as distinctly less than ideal. The reason why the NMPFT is a success, apart from the fact that it is a unique attraction in the UK, is fairly obvious: it communicates about and through media which a present day audience finds appealing and approachable. At the time it opened, the NMPFT was arguably the most interactive museum presentation in the UK. To put it in context, though, it should be said that the cité des Sciences et de l'Industrie at la Villette in Paris easily surpasses it in terms of successful communication. It should also be noticed that even such a 'high-culture' city as Paris has recognized the need to communicate its history to visiting tourists in a mass market way through the idiosyncratically romantic film presentation 'Paristoric', referred to already. This is shown on the hour, 365 days a year, accompanied by commentary in a range of languages.

In the UK, if only for financial reasons, brought about through a change in the focus of political culture, the need to rethink styles and methods of communication, to make them noticeably more effective has been recognized by most people involved in the 'heritage industry'. This applies even to the more esoteric museum circles although, for a variety of reasons, there were 'outposts' remaining at the end of the heritage industry decade. It had become obvious to the majority of museums and sites that the information they had at their disposal could be explained more easily and to a wider audience if it was communicated in a way that that audience found **entertaining**. For a money-making cultural site to be lucrative, unless a very high spend per capita could be expected for some particular reason, it was necessary for it to be attractive and that included the style of presentation, plus the add-on facilities like restaurants and shops. Emblematic among national museum revamps in the UK encapsulating new communications styles are those of the National Maritime Museum, which has a new Twentieth Century Sea Power gallery featuring 'a nine screen audio-visual diplay,'[9] and the Natural History Museum where there are 'robot dinosaurs . . . interactive video quizzes and computer animations'. The head of PR at the latter museum, Dr Roger Miles, emphasizes that 'education comes first and presentation second'. Miles told Hugh Pearman: 'We always start by thinking what we want to say. Only then do we consider how we are going to say it. But we *are* trying to communicate science in a way that is relevant to visitors' own lives.'

Multi-media communications techniques range from the already relatively routine interactive compact disc system to virtual reality, a process, born of flight simulation, still undergoing development and refinement.[10] Between the two extremes are a variety of developments, ranging from the relatively technically simple visitor experience to items of considerable sophistication, both technically and in terms of their characteristics of reality. Virtual reality, whose development is driven principally by the demands of the games industry, is also being used as an overtly educational tool. In the autumn of 1991 the Australian Jeffrey Shaw's VR 'Le Musée Virtuel' was displayed in the Attelier du Virtuel at the 'Machines à Communiquer' exhibition at the cité des Sciences et de l'Industrie. Also, for a three-day period, admission was free to all the cité's exhibits. In 1993 at the Imagina conference, generally regarded as a showcase of the most bow-wave introductions, a monk's tour of 11th-century Cluny Abbey in televirtuality was on show. A VR trip to a temple at Luxor (likely to be much safer than a real visit) has been developed by the Japanese. A company called Black Dog Productions has produced 'Virtual Egypt' which 'combines surrogate travel with excursions into the mythology of ancient Egypt'.[11] From spring 1994, VR was scheduled to be shown in Rome at the Museum of Roman Civilisation. And this is just the beginning.

87

Of course developing a virtual world raises a lot of issues.[12] It is reported that 'Psychologists are particularly interested in VR because they want to find out how easy it is to "fool" the human mind into thinking it is actually in the virtual world.'[13] With regard to education, Cotton and Brown devote a section in their book specifically to the educational applications of hypermedia, beginning it with the assessment: 'The impact of hypermedia in education is likely to be the most controversial of all the application areas we examine ... as well as offering a promise of positive change that will improve the quality of education for all, hypermedia also represents a threat to the traditions, values and practices that have grown up over the years.'[14]

This chapter has sought to demonstrate that almost cataclysmic changes are in process. They are not confined, of course, to the field of education but are occurring in society in general. However, the educational changes are particularly well pronounced because that subject's main focus is the young, representing the new generation, as guided and informed by the less young, the older generation; together with a consideration of the type and content of the information matter that is transmitted (or not) between young and less young. A comment by the Chair of Women in Computing, Helen Watt, is relevant here. According to a *Guardian* report,[15] she said, 'There is no doubt that computing at all levels is failing to attract women.' Not only, therefore, might there be a **horizontal division by generation** in information transmission to be addressed, but also a **vertical split by gender**.

5 The material and aims for communication

The method of education used at or about a cultural site is only one of two aspects of information. This channel of communication is one aspect, but *what* is communicated is one of the issues that is most challenging and difficult. As has been demonstrated in regard to various cultural sites in various countries, often the most 'bow-wave' and sophisticated response on an issue is likely to have come from the direction of Paris' cité des Sciences et de l'Industrie at la Villette. As the cité's President says, in his Introduction to the *Guide to the Permanent Exhibition Explora*,[16] 'The message we want to get across could be summed up by a word to the wise: "Don't blindly entrust experts with the fate of future generations."' This passage transmits empowerment, the essence of all education and information communication. The concept of empowerment is central to this chapter and is therefore a suitable item with which to conclude it.

Issues and questions

* Communication styles between young and old.
* Range of audience knowledge levels.
* Virtuality.
* Reinterpretation and evaluation.
* 'New' audiences.

a) What are the main audience groups at a tourist site and what are their distinguishing characteristics in communications terms?
b) Is it possible to communicate to a mass audience simultaneously and if so, how?
c) How can information about a site be made compelling and interesting to people round the world?

Further reading

Centre for Environmental Education, *Visitors Welcome*, English Heritage, London, HMSO, 1988.

Tabata, R., Yamashiro, J. and Cherem, G. (eds) Proceedings of the Heritage Interpretation International Third Global Congress, *Joining Hands for Quality Tourism: Interpretation, Preservation and the Travel Industry*, Honolulu, University of Hawaii, 1992.

Issues of the USA magazine, *Wired*, and from March 1995 of the UK edition.

3.4

Entertaining

In Chapter 3.3, appropriate ways of educating and informing about cultural sites were considered. The emphasis was upon communicating relevant knowledge effectively, in a way that would be as compelling as possible, and in that context, therefore, how to entertain was considered. The aim, though, was not to show how to entertain directly, but rather how to use entertaining methods when communicating for the purposes of education and information dissemination. This chapter's aim, on the other hand, takes as a primary objective how to make a cultural site entertaining for a visitor in a way that is appropriate to that particular site.

1 Enjoyment at sites

Example: The Pont du Gard, France

One of the places at which the public can be seen having the most entertaining time without doing any obvious harm to a historic monument is at the Pont du Gard, a World Heritage Site, in southern France (see also Chapter 2.3). On a warm, late summer's day, as the massive Roman aqueduct comes into view, delighted squeals and splashes can be heard from the direction of the idly running river below. A mass of sunbathers on the exposed river gravels soak up the late summer sun, a happy scene with no perceptible threat to the Pont du Gard. That people had gathered there specifically meant, presumably, that they saw some particular benefit in being near the historic aqueduct; it was interesting that they were there rather than at the coast. The Pont du Gard was being used, quite appropriately, as a backdrop to 20th-century fun.

2 Why and how to create an enjoyable experience

As has been indicated in Chapter 2.1, the reasons people go to historic sites are many and various. If people go to sites, as surely the majority of them must, with the aim of deriving enjoyment from the experience, how can this be delivered appropriately? If the avowed intention of a presenter is to get a message across, and **if the experience of absorbing information is made enjoyable for the visitor, the process will occur all the more easily.** If, first and foremost, an enjoyable experience has been provided for visitors, they may also acquire a lot of information as part of it; had it been presented to them as a purely educational experience, they might have stayed away.

Heritage stories and themes provide marvellous material for entertainment, because of their **innate differentness** from 20th-century daily life. They seem so 'other' that they and their images are as good as myths, legends and fairy tales for providing fantastic experiences. For some promoters, that history is history or that a site is old is not really the point: the point is that it looks different, quaint or picturesque. If a site is not perceived as adequately visually exciting or novel, then the instinct nowadays may be to vamp it up a bit, for example by dressing up in period costume, staging medieval banquets or mock battles, jousting, giving displays of falconry or producing a creepy dungeon display. In trying to be entertaining, some historic sites and museums may occasionally encroach on the territory of theme parks. In a desperate effort to provide the proverbial family day out, a mish-mash of facilities can develop, not all of them sympathetic or appropriate to the site and its character. Yet, very often, entertainment adds to the spirit of a place and augments a site's ability to communicate its particular meaning and role. Making the necessary mental leap across centuries sometimes requires some assistance. Events and entertainments can help bring a site alive to its visitors.

Example: National Trust fêtes champêtres

These events at certain National Trust sites cater to the whim to dress up and have picnics, and are in their design and conduct suitable to their sites. They help convey the 'presence' of a site, at an unusual and especially atmospheric time of day, for they are night occasions. They also generate extra income for sites' upkeep.

Provided they are chosen appropriately, such attractions and entertainments as *son et lumières*, music concerts of various types, plays, dance, poetry readings, etc., only serve to enhance sites. The great benefit too is that they attract regular new adherents to visiting these historic sites, by the provision of what is an add-on attraction: a subject area will have a separate audience of its own so a new group can be introduced to a site.

3 Presentations by ethnic groups

A problem with cultural entertainment which features live presentation by ethnic groups of aspects of their culture – native dances, displays of folk crafts and customs, etc. – may be that, during the process of entertaining tourists, the human dignity of the performers can come perilously close to disappearing. If the performers are trying to earn a living from the activity they are, ostensibly, in an instrinsically weak position, even though they will probably at least have the strength of being on home ground. So-called 'natives' are potentially easy victims in the game of entertaining westernized tourists who, due to their wealth and 'education', are likely to be 'in the driving seat' in the situation. It has to be said that some such 'native' entertainment displays can possess constituents that render them inappropriate as items of cultural tourism. The main message at the Global Conference, *Building a Sustainable World Through Tourism*, in 1994, was that for the exchange between a tourist and his service provider to be appropriate and fruitful, there ought broadly to be a *balanced* exchange between them, not a situation of exploitation of one by the other. This applies generally, as well as to the circumstances described above.

4 Stimulation and sensation

When we look for entertainment at a site, essentially we are looking for heightened sensation, a 'buzz'. What will represent that sensation for an audience will be as different as our tastes. From the newer entertainment attractions in the heritage field, it is possible to gain an impression of by what means presenters believe we seek and achieve sensation: performance, seeing roles enacted or acting roles ourselves, as in a range of types of contest, battles, teacher–pupil dialogues, produces excitement and interest, for example. With these, such presenters seem to seek to offer life with an exclamation mark.

5 Characteristics of entertaining sites

In perusing the promotional material for four of the UK's principal new heritage attractions – the one 'Award winning', another 'Voted Visitor Attraction of the Year', and two others from Heritage (in its earlier guise, the celebrated Heritage Projects) – certain key words and phrases are encountered. From these, it is possible to obtain a sense – to use a not inappropriate word – of the character of definition of these attractions. Among words and phrases that occur are: 'thrill, challenge, stimulate', 'light, sound and smells!', 'see, feel, hear and do!', 'play an active part', 'entertaining and educational', 'fun and excitement for everyone', 'educational and entertaining, but most of all – it is fun!'. Reviewing 'Les Martyrs de Paris', a new attraction from the team which produced the Dungeons at London and York, Patrick Weber asked 'Where are we? In one of those tourist attractions where sensation-seekers can satisfy their morbid cravings by immersing themselves in the murkier aspects of history . . . the martyrs of the past make good scapegoats for today's ghouls.'[1]

6 *Does seeking to entertain lead presenters to go too far?*

Should we regard such activities as inappropriate or see them as harmless and suitable aids to stimulating curiosity about the past and opening up routes to it which would otherwise never have been found, still less explored? Is a message debased by being made entertaining? Journalist Hugh Pearman, reviewing two exhibitions, one from France but showing in Glasgow, called 'Home of the Brave', and another, 'Pirates – Fact and Fiction', at the National Maritime Museum, considered the 'very fine line between the populist cultural show that succeeds in conveying its message, and the populist cultural show that fails'.[2] The former exhibition aimed high whereas the latter did not, according to Pearman. Both pulled in the crowds – and this is Pearman's point: 'You can draw the crowds *and* keep your integrity.'

7 *To be entertaining or not*

It is easy to deride entertainment's role in cultural communication, and criticize the heritage industry for its popularization of culture and cultural sites. A visit to a part of the world where the tentacles of the heritage industry have yet to reach is salutary. It is a reminder that perhaps something has been lost in the effort to popularize and to communicate through entertainment; but it also reminds us how much has been gained.

Example: Hungary

Overall, visits to Hungary's sites and museums are a salutary experience, acting as a reminder of what such places, for example in the UK, often used to be like. The visitor from a westernized country may long for the whole panoply of user-friendly facilities and information that have come to be regarded as the norm for site and museum visits in the west. Such a tourist may yearn for a little glitzy presentation, some modern information boards, custodians who aren't dressed in drap nylon overalls, a few audio-visual displays, a good shop on site or just a decent place to have a cup of coffee.

Having said this, the example of Hungary's National Museum of Agriculture in Budapest, with its sheer astringency, air of respect for knowledge, sense that learning needs to be achieved and that to do so requires effort, its general air of earnestness, lack of glamour, and the basic quality of its exhibits, may be what makes it a memorable and appealing experience for the visitor. To have put in smells, a ghost train, or something similar would have been to insult its integrity and utterly inappropriate. On the whole, though, in Hungary, the lack of easily available, easily assimilable and well-presented information produces what appear to be wasted opportunity after wasted opportunity for potential communication.

8 Appropriate entertainment

The crucial factor when producing entertainment at a site, as has been suggested, is to determine what entertainment will enhance, not reduce, a site's meaning or stature. At its best, entertainment is not a mere diversion but a vehicle for creating greater knowledge, understanding and awareness, joy and uplift. Entertainment can help bring out the best in a site, or show its hidden depths. Small plane, glider or balloon trips over sites are instances of what can be appropriately entertaining ways to view them. They literally provide a new perspective. A cruise on a lake should also be diverting, and it too would offer a different 'angle'. However, a restored boat, such as the steam yacht which tours Lake Coniston in the Lake District, gives an extra dimension of interest to the entertainment of the experience, because of its historical authenticity.

When considering ways of educating at a site or museum in Chapter 3.3, some technological devices for communicating information were described. Many of these are part of the entertaining experience of a site: in entertaining they inform.

The heritage industry was criticized for using heritage as a vehicle for entertainment. It might seem that images from history were merely adopted for use in entertainment because they looked picturesque and strangely different, rather than for what they meant or represented as history. But the industry can equally be praised (as in the example of absence in Hungary, mentioned above), for attracting a whole new audience of visitors, by making sites entertaining and therefore approachable. Often in the heritage industry the entertainment has got out of hand, or has been wholly inappropriate from the outset, but though some criticism may be justified in relation to accusations of rampant 'theme parkery', it should not be forgotten that these methods have attracted new audiences for history and for historical sites and collections.

9 The evolution of site entertainment

Perhaps colonial Williamsburg in Virginia, which started to be established in new mode in the inter-war era, was the first historical site to be made positively entertaining. Here, 'dressed-up' attendants and demonstrations of traditional skills are among the devices used to help visitors enjoy the process of trying to relate to and understand an era other than their own.

Example 1: Ironbridge Gorge Museum

In the UK, this entertaining style of history began to be used from the 1970s, with the establishment of Ironbridge Gorge as a museum. Ironbridge's most entertaining and controversial aspect and, it should be said, the most crowd-pulling as well was Blists Hill, a creation of old buildings – some erected on new territory, some not – together with a number of entirely new 'old' buildings. In line with the custom at many an authentic historic site in the USA, the staff at Blists Hill wear period costume and act out historical roles for visitors' erudition and entertainment.

Example II: North of England Open Air Museum

Similar activity to that described above was meanwhile occurring at the North of England Open Air Museum at Beamish. The collections for this museum began to be assembled by Frank Atkinson, its founder, in the 1960s.

Example III: Arbeia

Recreation *in situ* has been tried out at a Roman site near South Shields, in the UK. A controversial decision was taken, in an area of high unemployment, to construct a west gate at the Roman fort of Arbeia, as it might have looked in the Roman period, upon the original west gate's foundations. On high days and holidays, support to its appearance is given by the presence of a guard of men dressed up in appropriate costume for the period.

Example IV: Berlin

So appealing to some is the polyester sheeting and scaffolding Schloss in former East Berlin (described in Chapter 3.1), put up temporarily and regarded by those who disapproved of it as 'a crude Disney-style publicity stunt', that some demands are being made that it be re-created in more permanent and substantial form.

When considering heritage that is entertaining, it should be remembered that theatricality and pastiche have been present in cultural forms, overt follies among them, down the ages. Many of them are among the most deeply regarded heritage items nowadays.

10 In summary

Entertainment at a site or museum often gives it a necessary zest and provides a vital stimulus to that place's recognition in historical terms. The concern must be, however, that the entertainment should be appropriate, accentuating the presence and meaning of a site, not demeaning it.

Issues and questions

* Sensation.
* Dignity.
* Ethnic presentations.
* New perspectives.

a) What might be the benefits of using entertaining methods at a site?
b) What types of entertainment might be appropriate in attracting tourists to which type of site?
c) Can entertainment affect a site?

Further reading

Waters, I., *Entertainment, Arts and Cultural Services*, Second Edition, Harlow, Longman/Institute of Leisure and Amenity Management, 1994.

3.5

Commercializing

To produce a situation that is commercially lucrative to a presenter, it is necessary not only to encourage people to visit a site but also to create an environment in which they are persuaded that it is worthwhile paying for the experience. The ways and means of doing this, in a manner that is appropriate to the circumstances, is this chapter's subject.

1 Ways and means

Often the automatic assumption by some presenters is that a good financial return will need to be obtained through the 'gate'. While this may often be so, it can be far better in some situations to have a low or non-existent fee for admittance to get people to come to a site. This may be with the straight aim of increasing visitor throughput, or with the purpose of providing other attractions to tempt expenditure once customers are over a site's threshold. Side attractions may achieve higher expenditure per capita than could be obtained at a site's entry point without causing the 'turn-off' that might occur there. Once an audience has been achieved, a mood to spend can be generated as result of being at a site and experiencing its aura. On the other hand, a high entry fee can generate an air of exclusivity about a site, and is likely to produce a market segment of people who are wealthy or have a higher than average disposable income or who are extremely keen to see the site. If goods are provided at a site shop, or food is served at its café or restaurant, which are suitably upmarket to suit a clientèle that is particularly discriminating in such areas of its lifestyle, or if a sense of 'once in lifetime so we won't stint ourselves' is produced across the board, the spend per person can be high. It should be emphasized, however, that to keep a broad-based audience, in terms of categories of economic affluence and also therefore by implication those of social group, a low basic fee of admission needs to be the objective.

Example I: Buckingham Palace, London

Buckingham Palace has provided an exemplarily high quality of goods for sale. With the sense of specialness to a visit there, especially for those who come from long distances away overseas and who may never travel to London again, it would appear that Buckingham Palace has an audience which, though quite large and also wide in range of type, is in this particular situation disposed to be high-spending.

Albeit that the market here is in some ways very mixed, a message to be drawn is, essentially, that pricing can be used to select an audience. A 'specialness' of circumstance produces a situation of special, not everyday, spending to match. In general, **the techniques of the marketplace – pre-eminently the supermarket – are just as applicable in the creation and building up of a customer-base for a cultural attraction as for anything else.**

The use of 'brands' like the Tate and Guggenheim has been mentioned. Attractions like Club Med and some theme parks have shown the invitingness of the 'all in price' to certain sectors of the market. For some types of purchaser it is helpful to know that he need not be nervous about hidden or additional costs and he may pay quite dearly initially to achieve this assurance. Pricing can also govern an audience's size, often usefully. Fewer people means less site damage, and if spend per person is increased fewer people need not mean a consequent loss of some revenue.

Example II: Strengths, weaknesses, opportunities, threats

A useful and necessary exercise in analysing the qualities of a cultural attraction that are likely to appeal is to conduct what in marketing terms is called a SWOT analysis. This process seeks to define what are the direct strengths and weaknesses of a 'product' – the site in this instance – and to assess its opportunities and threats in terms of its relation with its external environment.

As has been indicated, when assessing the commercial potential of a cultural site it would be necessary to identify: its distinctive characteristics, for example, a unique collection of Russian books; and then its disadvantages, no room for temporary exhibitions, say. Then, in analysing the external circumstances, one might find that: to its advantage, it was near a bus station and in a centre of population; to its disadvantage, it was in a town with a sizeable Estonian community, was a long way from an international communication-link node, and it was in an area of poverty and high unemployment. It is easy to see from this what it would be appropriate and inappropriate to focus on, and what could be envisaged as the site's most appropriate audience in both commercial and other terms.

2 Difficult situations for earning revenue

Example I: Inaccessibility to a prime audience

Compensatory factors for any defects need to be identified. An example of an ostensibly difficult cultural site on which to capitalize is the collection of Andy Warhol-iana in an old communist centre in a small Czech town near the painter's birthplace. The best commercial option for the presenter would seem to be to publicize and operate a strong mail order system to generate revenue.

Example II: Sensitive situations

Sometimes it is simply not regarded as appropriate to make commercial capital from a cultural attraction, at some religious sites for example. Though certain Christian cathedrals have decided positively to request voluntary donations, most cathedrals or churches at least provide the opportunity in the form of a donation box for the collection of alms for repair and maintenance of their fabric or for charitable purposes. At Christian sites which are still being used for religious purposes, however, there is a general reluctance to be overtly commercial in what is regarded as God's house. A solution here, as in other instances where it is judged inappropriate to sell or make money on site, is to make an add-on provision, at a location where commercial activity *would* be appropriate. At the World Heritage Site of Chartres Cathedral, a new museum is being built at its front. It will be interesting to see what type of commercial operation occurs there, if any.

3 High quality and standards

The main message from the commercial sector of society which also applies in the particular context of cultural sites and the attempt to achieve financial benefit from them, is that in general people will pay a reasonable amount provided they are getting what they want. What they want, on the whole, quite understandably, is a **high standard of facility** for the relevant category of type. In western society the 1980s saw the general burgeoning of the service and retail sector, and this taught customers to expect as the norm good standards of presentation and quality of service. In general, in their leisure activities as in other facets of their lives, larger numbers of people expected facilities and resources of a higher level of excellence than hitherto. To compete successfully with other attractions providing leisure and spending opportunities, principally shopping malls, cultural sites and venues need to excel in what they offer or offer something different as a reason for attendance at them.

4 Promotion

As has been indicated, the right cultural attraction in the right place is a wonderful starting point in the pursuit of commercial activity at a site. A site will not be in the 'right' place, in terms of attracting an audience and market, unless that audience and market is aware of its existence and thus able to go to it. So marketing a site is necessary, in whatever way is deemed appropriate to that site and its projected audience.

5 The best response all round

Though the purpose of this book as a whole is to look at what could be considered appropriate activity in regard to a cultural site, it is necessary here to look at what might or might not be appropriate **commercial** activity for the site in question. The particular concerns of religious sites have been referred to already. In general, the ideal is that any commercial activity should be that which is most suitable simultaneously to meet the needs of a site, its presenter and its audience. Mismatches, where activity is inappropriate, spoiling the atmosphere of a place, simply 'grate'.

6 Types of 'selling point(s)'

Economic necessity may require that people and places must realize the commercial potential of their area. It has been suggested how that potential may be evaluated. Having understood the needs of a suitable market for a certain area, it should be possible to meet those needs appropriately. In terms of a site having an ability to be commercial, it appears everything has the potential. Even ostensibly quite nasty areas can be promoted and presented to catch a market. It is reported that 'Walking tours of sleazy areas such as Pigalle are popular',[1] and that some Swedes 'tired of London's more conventional attractions' are going on 'slum visits' of a north Peckham Council estate. Though no longer operating, the ultimate nasty–popular excursion might appear to have been 'Bob's Intifada Tours . . . which specialised in tours aimed at members of the American Jewish Defence League on holiday in Israel'. Bob, 'Packing his well-protected minibus with tourists . . . would drive deep into Palestinian settlements on the West Bank and Gaza Strip in the hope of provoking local residents into stoning the bus.'

It might have been anticipated that the set of the ill-fated television soap opera *Eldorado* would become a tourist attraction. Sure enough, even before the last reel of *Eldorado* had been shot, two-hour tours, at 1,500 pesetas a go, were in operation and T-shirts were being sold. An *Adios Eldorado* video was made for sale too.[2]

7 Indirect opportunities

Example I: Good associated facilities

In Italy, a country not previously at the top of the league in terms of considering the needs of the market for its cultural sites, an effort is now under way to make its state museums self-financing. The Italian Minister of Culture is reportedly 'convinced that there is a big market in museum-related products, such as books, cards, T-shirts and information packages'.[3] The Minister, Alberto Ronchey, has said that 'World-famous works of art should be able to maintain themselves.' If he can 'bring private enterprise into the museums with cafés, restaurants and cloakrooms', he hopes to encourage people 'to spend more time and money in the museum'.

Example II: The supporting attraction

Side attractions helping to support a main attraction are quite usual nowadays. One cultural attraction providing direct support to another, though in practice commonplace, is still not usually done in an overt and extended way. With the headline 'Van Gogh bails out Mondrian as Dutch slash arts subsidies'[4] the situation changed. The plan was for profits from a Van Gogh exhibition to pay for a proportion of the 1994 Piet Mondrian exhibition, and the decision was made in the context of increasing recession and of 'intense debate in the Dutch parliament on future funding of important cultural events'.

Example III: Being sure of meeting the sponsor's needs

During the boom years of the 1980s sponsors became the cultural heritage's traditional saviours and benefactors, but the recession did, of course, lead to pressure to generate financial support for culture and cultural events from other sources as well. In the harder times, sponsors became more discerning, and to still get their support, supplicants had to meet sponsors' needs that much more appropriately and well.

8 Causes and effects

As has been indicated, pricing at a high level may serve to exclude those with less wealth. This has apparently happened in Czechoslovakia, where in Prague prices at facilities like restaurants and pubs have risen to a level such that visitors can still afford them, but locals are priced out of the market, causing the development of a tourists' rather than a citizens' city.

Vermont in the USA on the other hand is determined not to fall victim to change brought about by greed. To protect itself, most particularly from a shopping mall invasion, the entire state was in 1993 put at the top of the '"endangered" historic places'[5] list produced annually by the National Trust for Historic Preservation.

9 The need for careful evaluation and assessment

Just as it has been assessed as inappropriate for Vermont to go overboard for commercial gain, so it is necessary to evaluate the level and type of commercial activity that may or may not be appropriate at the rest of the world's cultural sites. As has been indicated, what may be quite acceptable in one situation will be utterly unsuitable and inappropriate elsewhere. If the commercial activity associated with a cultural site does not allow that site to stay true to its essence and type, it will have sold itself short in a fundamental and damaging way. This holds true for even a single cultural item. Unfortunately, examples are legion of the inappropriate representation of cultural images on products for commercial purposes. Recently obtainable from London's Museum Shop was a '50 inch high plastic blow-up' of the figure depicted in Edvard Munch's painting 'The Scream'.

In summary

It must be emphasized that if a site is to attract visitors, and therefore potential sources of income, it must represent a more desirable location for leisure activity than any other of a variety of attractive opportunities available.

Issues and questions

* Market-place approach and techniques.
* Sensitive situations.
* Standards.

a) Are there types of site which are not suitable to be treated as commercial commodities?
b) How can a site be evaluated for visitor attractiveness and revenue-generating capacity?
c) If a site is not able to operate as a commercial enterprise itself, how might income for it be generated?

Further reading

Laws, E., *Tourism Marketing: Service and Quality Management Perspectives*, Cheltenham, Stanley Thornes (Publishers) Ltd, 1991.
Ohmae, K., *The Borderless World: Power and Strategy in the Interlinked Economy*, London, Collins, 1990; London, Fontana, 1992.

Part 4
Conclusion

4.1

Cultural tourism now and for the future

Tourism: a world industry demanding concerted world-wide action for its suitable management

The Earth Summit in Rio, held in 1992, was referred to in Part 1. This crisis meeting sought to address world problems which threaten us to the level of extinction. Tourism, which is well on the way to becoming the world's largest industry, was not on the agenda. Shortly before the Summit opened Desmond Balmer, Travel Editor of *The Observer* newspaper, reported: 'Tourism is not on the agenda of the Rio Earth Summit. Politicians already run the risk of doing too little too late on global pollution, yet they will not even be talking about a problem that threatens to be as significant.'[1]

In this book, an attempt has been made to suggest what matters should be featuring on an agenda for appropriate cultural tourism. Throughout the discussion, the endeavour has been to make clear that, if we are to manage cultural tourism appropriately, it is no use just opening a site to the public without thought and then complaining if it is misused. We need to evaluate carefully the likely needs of a site and decide how to meet them appropriately or, where necessary, how to discourage inappropriate use.

It is a pity that the Earth Summit did not take a lead by considering tourism specifically. In tourism we have a world item to address. It is fairly obvious that a world industry will require world involvement in its management. Using data from the World Health Organisation, the World Resources Institute, the World Bank, the UN Population Fund, the UN Environment Programme and the UN Development Programme, *The Sunday Times* produced a world map[2] in advance of the Summit, alongside an article entitled 'The View from the Summit' which did at least identify the threat to the Alps from tourism (see Chapters 2.3 and 3.2). At the Summit, 'the emergence of Japan as a world environmental superpower'[3] was seen. Following an opinion poll, an erstwhile Japanese environment minister attributed to 'the lifestyle of the north' a role as 'one of the causes of today's environmental destruction'.

In an issue of *WTO News: Tourism Policy Trends and Perspectives*,[4] the Secretary-General of the World Tourism Organization addressed tourism problems quite squarely. Antonio Enriquez Savignac said, 'The international tourism industry faces a menu of medium-term issues and a series of challenges that must be met for the industry to consolidate properly. Foremost is the need to translate the multi-disciplinary requirements of tourism into systems, processes and partnerships that can have global application.' He continued, 'With tourism conservatively projected to grow by about 50 per cent over the next seven to eight years, many of the problems we now face and will continue to face require **global management and co-operation.**'

An exemplary role for World Heritage Sites

I would suggest first of all, therefore, that, as world representatives, all the World Heritage Sites have a special obligation to take a lead, to show themselves to be world models, in the appropriate management of cultural sites for tourism.

Trends and themes

We must address the issue of how we are to manage cultural tourism appropriately. So far in this book I have tried to define how this might be done. Now I would like to identify, first, some of the emerging trends and themes that will affect what the characteristics of the response might appropriately be. Then I would like to offer a perspective on what I believe may come to be the most appropriate, not to say radical, response in a number of instances.

1 Europe: first in cultural tourism

In his book, *Tourism in Europe*,[5] Rob Davidson says, 'In terms of international tourism, Europe is not only the *origin* of most tourists, but also the *destination* for most international travellers.' He goes on to say 'Despite being the second smallest of the seven continents, Europe attracts far more international tourists and more spending on international tourism than any other continent.' Turning to cultural heritage specifically, he says,

> Undoubtedly, the rich and varied cultural heritage of Europe is instrumental in attracting visitors from other parts of the world, as well as motivating Europeans themselves to travel around their own, and neighbouring, countries. Many of the continent's museums, monuments, art galleries, palaces, and cathedrals enjoy a worldwide reputation. . . . 'Cultural tourism' of this kind is the motivation behind the vast majority of visits to Europe from the less ancient continents of the 'New World', and also plays a major part in the growing trend towards the taking of short breaks and second holidays.

There is no respite predicted here for the European heritage sites overloaded with tourists. Maybe Europeans themselves underestimate, because they take it for granted, their heritage and its pulling power. Michael Ignatieff believes 'the Europe we [Europeans] care about most remains the Europe of Christendom'. He says,

> Now the body of Christendom is gone but its skeleton remains, the white bleached stones of its buildings. This is the skeleton which still holds us upright. . . . Christian Europe was also peasant Europe. . . . In the next two generations an age-old European culture will disappear, leaving behind a museum culture of the anonymous labour that made us what we are. . . . The passing of peasant Europe and Christendom leaves us in a culture of consumption that we share with the rest of the world but which we really cannot call our own.[6]

Perhaps, as Peter Millar has suggested in *The European*,[7] a European Heritage Fund is needed to care for the European heritage. He puts forward the idea that 'There could be a "friends of Europe" club, open to Japanese and Americans too, which would charge annual membership in exchange for free entry to everything from the Eiffel Tower to the Leaning Tower of Pisa.' Nice thought, but would these better conserved sites be visited more as a result, in which case would the club be of any use to the cultural site? Would the club just be funding its own accommodation at sites, so to speak? Whatever the solution to their conservation, the cultural sites of Europe remain high on the tourist agenda for the future because of their popularity with the world's tourists.

2 Training and education

It is recognized that there needs to be more training of tourism staff. In Europe, the Hotel, Catering and Institutional Management Association has set out 'to identify the future qualification needs of managers in Europe's tourism industry' and 'has been . . . active in a lobby of the European Parliament . . . to campaign, through the European Tourism Intergroup, for the need to establish Europe-wide standards of education and training in the hospitality sector'.[8] In Britain, the Travel and Tourism Programme, originally set up in 1988 by business partners who included Forte Hotels and American Express, has the aim of 'raising student awareness of the importance of the tourism industry'[9] and has helped in the development of the GCSE Travel and Tourism course. The Programme has served as a model for similar initiatives in places like Hong Kong, Mexico, Hungary and France. The WTO and the George Washington University have established jointly the International Institute of Tourism Studies, a centre for post-graduate level study with programmes embracing education, research and management development. The University has established a Tourism 2000 Summer Tourism Institute covering development and management matters.

Education in sites' needs is, of course, paramount if the conduct of cultural tourism is to be appropriate. While adult training in a range of practical conservation and management skills is available, it is vital to develop an understanding and appreciation on the part of the public at large about how and why a cultural site needs to be cared for and managed in relation to tourist visits. In the UK, the issues are addressed in publications for the young from a range of conservation bodies with properties visited by the tourist, including English Heritage and the National Trust.

3 The appropriation of tourism for outsiders' use and purposes

Tourism is in the spotlight. In recognition of its economic might and potential, it is now becoming used as a tool of persuasion. By menacing tourists and so threatening a country or group's tourism industry, terrorists, and those using other less extreme methods of approach, are hoping to bring political or other influence to bear. Their aim is to redress what are perceived as inequalities or unsuitabilities in society and their method is attack on what are seen as its more wealthy and influential representatives.

4 A cultural site: demands upon it for spiritual reasons and for meeting individual needs

Our approach to the management of cultural tourism sites has, in my view, failed to recognize adequately the spiritual needs that tourists may have of a site. While these may be religious in a formal sense, they may have other tones too. The entertainment industry has sometimes shown much greater recognition of our need for fantasy and dreams and catered to it than have other areas of society. The catchphrase of Fujitsu, leader in the VR entertainment field, is 'What Mankind Can Dream, Technology Can Achieve'.[10]

A temporary sight at the site at Bosworth Field in the UK where Richard III, 'the last Plantagenet King of England' (and in many quarters regarded as a 'baddie') was killed in battle brought home how deep and enduring our spiritual needs of a cultural tourism site may be. In front of the stone marking the site of the King's death was a withering floral tribute with a card attached upon which were written the words 'For "Dickon". Loyaulte Me Lie My Lord, The White Rose Always.' That a man dead for five centuries and more still had such relevance and meaning to someone today is extremely awesome.

In managing cultural tourism sites the impulse may be to package an attraction, for understandable reasons. It should be recognized, however, that in so doing, one cultural imprint (that which the package represents) is being imposed, in effect, upon all an attraction's activity. The point was, Arnold Wesker reported, made forcibly, though in a different context by Janet Daly on the Radio 4 programme 'The Moral Maze' when she said: 'The reasons that fascists and political totalitarians of all kinds hate culture is because it heightens people's awareness of themselves as individuals. It gives them the internal resources to resist conformity; and it's ultimately as necessary to a free society as the vote or private property and it's deeply wicked to deprive people of the right to a way into the life of the mind.'[11]

5 Cultural mix and separation

For freedom of thought and the freedom to be different to be ever present requires acceptance of individuality and multi-culturalism as the norm. In an *International Herald Tribune* report of a speech given by George Yong-Boon Yeo, Singapore Minister for Information and the Arts, at the World Economic Forum in Davos, he was described as saying, 'To cut off a person's past, the way African slave owners did, is terribly crippling. Like trees, humans cannot grow without roots.... Cultures will converge to some degree as the world shrinks, but cultural and religious differences will not disappear. No amount of Western influence will make Japanese or Chinese society Western or vice versa. What we should seek is to make multi-culturalism a part of every culture.'[12] In this context, the comments about Tokyo and Los Angeles by Simon Winchester in his book *The Pacific* are interesting. He observes of Tokyo, 'It had managed to absorb the essence of the world without for a moment diluting its true self, its ineffable sense of the Japanese identity.... The very opposite is true of Los Angeles.'[13]

6 The past, technology and change

Throughout this book, I have sought to chart how society is changing. We are now at a special and important turning point. The change in society is, in the main, being brought about by technology. A sea change can be sensed in the way that we are starting to perceive our cultural monuments. It seems we are witnessing the emergence of a more genuine form of democracy, wrought through easy availability of information to a far wider society than at any time past. How we regard the cultural artefacts of the past will reflect this changing attitude.

This change of attitude was perhaps first acknowledged overtly in relation to the fire at Windsor Castle. The Castle is a symbol of royalty and while it continued to be highly regarded in its society, it could be construed that that society was still in some way elitist and not yet truly democratic in character. Yet, writing a little while after the official end of royalty's *annus horribilis*, Deyan Sudjic suggested that the era of the general public accepting being told what to do with old things by heritage industry official gurus was at an end. He said, 'The fire at Windsor Castle may in retrospect prove to have been the watershed, marking an end to the knee-jerk response that new automatically meant worse.'[14]

The past is a source of enrichment, inspiration and stimulation, for the present and the future. It does not serve society at large, and cultural tourists among it, well if it acts as a constraint and dampener upon new thoughts, approaches and action. The UK is an example of a nation whose past has featured so largely in general contemporary activity as to reduce new thought and creativity.

I believe we are seeing the end to our living in an old society and our entry into a new one. In this book, I have drawn attention to the generational difference and the relationship to it of the role and relevance of computers in people's lives. In his seminal book, *Generation X*, which offers so many acute descriptions of attitude ascribed to the generation he discusses, Douglas Coupland portrays the activity of 'Historical Slumming: the act of visiting locations such as diners, smokestack industrial sites, rural villages – locations where time appears to have been frozen many years back – so as to experience relief when one returns back to "the present" '.[15]

I referred in Chapter 3.3 to the so-called *otaku* kids in Japan. The feelings of a western parent have been described by Carolyn Roden, who said: 'my son is a computer games hermit, emerging only to be fed and watered . . . my son and his peers seem to find just living in the present moment tedious unless it is masked by a Walkman plugged into eager ears, a hand-held computer game or the full fix of the computer terminal punching at full volume. This is supplemented by the ever-active television placed a foot or two from the terminal, so that any transitory moments of boredom, such as when a game is loading up, can be alleviated by a dose of cartoons.'[16]

Throughout the book it has been strongly suggested that to manage cultural tourism appropriately it will be necessary to adopt modern methods. Researchers in Japan, led by Professor Tadahiro Omi, have now developed a ' "super intelligent logic system" which can retrieve data as fast as the human brain'.[17] The ultimate in 'intelligent' buildings has been developed in Japan too. Architect Yoshinobu Ashihara has commented, 'I imagine that Parisians look upon the intense energy and apparent confusion of cities in Japan like Tokyo with a mixture of contempt and envy. The coming twenty-first century will be an era of sophisticated information technology. It will be necessary to lay optical fiber and lines for the information network system beneath the streets in our cities and to channel them to every part of our buildings. Will a city like Paris, where fundamental architectural change is impossible, be able to adapt? Perhaps we will all be compelled to re-evaluate the merits of the amoeba-like changefulness of a city like Tokyo.'[18] The question seems to be whether this new way of life can be accommodated in purely physical terms within and as part of the built fabric from the past we retain as our inheritance today. In relation to cultural tourism, it has to be asked whether we can manage to retain these historic items as places to be visited in the face of progress and its demands.

Emerging characteristics in cultural tourism management

Of the characteristics emerging in the practice of cultural tourism among those of major importance and significance are:

i) Since cultural tourism occurs across the world, its appropriate conduct must be considered globally.

ii) The basis for the above must be appropriate good management.

iii) This management must recognize that society is undergoing great changes.

iv) A major dimension of the change is the considerable difference between those with an easy familiarity with computers and computer-related activity and those with little or no computer literacy that now pertains.

v) Society will be multi-cultural.

vi) Democratization produces a mass tourism market rather than an elite tourism market.

vii) The need is to achieve sustainability.

viii) The religious and spiritual aspects of cultural tourism sites are strongly significant.

ix) With the growing recognition of the economic importance of tourism to nations, factions or groups has come the emergence of the threat to tourists of being victimized or terrorized for political or other gain.

x) An increase in social tourism has come about because of the emergence as tourists of people from various disadvantaged groups, producing a growing First/Third World disparity.

xi) The tourism load should be spread more evenly, both geographically and throughout the year.

xii) Europe will continue to be the main destination for the world's tourists.

xiii) There is a new emphasis on rural tourism.

xiv) New, modern solutions and methods are necessary.

xv) Technology is of vital importance.

xvi) Increasingly, information will be communicated in visual rather than verbal form.

xvii) Training and education are highly important.

It is interesting to see that the four main issue areas that are identified by the WTO Secretary General in relation to the management of global tourism are: '1) Statistics, indicators and information exchange; 2) Planning, development and management; 3) Technology; 4) Professionalism.'[19]

I have stressed the need for producing modern solutions to what is a modern situation, i.e. mass cultural tourism. The solutions to the management of the past lie in the future. Perhaps Potsdamer Platz in Berlin has an exemplary function in its special position as the reconfigured centre of a significant European city being subject to major redevelopment. Although the area is not yet regenerated, however, perhaps its time has already passed again?

If we are to manage our cultural tourism sites and items appropriately, to benefit the whole world, our solutions, I believe, have to be extremely radical and require a shift in 'mind-set'. There are untold masses of potential cultural tourists. To manage sites appropriately and effectively we have to change our attitude to them.

The first option, and a practice already in use in Japan, is to cultivate the frame of mind which focuses on **the idea** of a cultural item rather than its physical representation in original form. I referred earlier to the Ise Shrine, one of Japan's most venerated historic monuments, which is replaced every twenty years.[20] Of course, providing a replica rather than the 'real' thing does not, by itself, solve the problem of wear and tear from a mass of tourists converging upon a place. It does, however, allow the possibility of producing *several* replicas which could then be placed strategically at different locations which could accommodate them and large audiences. The other option, even more radical, requires an attitude of mind that **no longer requires travel to a site at all**, preferring to see its image replicated on TV, video disc or hologram, or experience it through virtual reality.

With either of these options, the impediment is overcoming preoccupations both with authenticity of fabric, in terms of having the 'right' age, of being the original, and with addressing a concept's physical manifestation rather than the concept itself. At the Shiretoko Snow Festival at Uturo Port in Japan, tourists are entertained with a laser aurora borealis since real sightings are 'extremely rare'.[21] Of course, if a person once becomes interested not in preserving historic fabric but in the continuation of an idea, a lot of the problems of cultural tourism today would be solved. As I have already suggested (Chapter 3.2), if the Pennine Way were to be regarded as a concept rather than a particular route on the ground, difficulties with parts being worn out could be easily solved by rerouting, without creating visitor disappointment. Of course, new paths are being made to lessen loads on existing ones quite a lot in the world but, as far as I know, no one has ever dared to call a new route near an old one by the latter's name in the way that the Japanese call a new Ise Shrine *the* Ise Shrine.

Many cultural sites across the world are already showing signs of wear and tear, spoiling their quality. In the interests of tourism they are losing their **integrity** too. As Douglas Coupland has said, 'If you ever have a free moment, you might consider checking out the travel brochures for the town in which you live. You might be amazed. You might not want to live there any more.'[22] Soon, I believe, if tourists are not better catered for at sites, if *they* do not have a quality time, they will react against the experience of visiting those sites and decide to stay away anyway. As Shintaro Ishihara has projected, in another context, but with a certain relevance here, 'In the future, political parties must stress the interests of consumers over those of producers, or risk rejection by the voters.'[23]

Good signs

Signs are beginning to emerge that the world is learning that it must manage its, fast becoming most major, industry better, and to more positive universal purpose. For a start, following the Earth Summit, there is much active work being done on Agenda 21.

At the 1994 International Institute for Peace through Tourism [IIPT] Global Conference, 'Building a Sustainable World Through Tourism', delegates were strongly united in recognizing the need to address and achieve success in managing tourism to achieve sustainability. There was also overall and widespread belief in tourism's huge potential for benefiting mankind and acting as an agent for peaceful co-existence. As was said in Chapter 3.3, Canada is among countries suggesting what approaches should be to tourism management. One useful lead showing tourists and the industry how sustainable tourism might be achieved is that of the Tourism Industry Association of Canada and the National Round Table on the Environment and the Economy in publishing their *Code of Ethics and Guidelines for Sustainable Tourism*.[24] The Chairman of the World Travel and Tourism Council at the IIPT Conference, which was held in Montreal, said that there would be 348 million jobs in the travel and tourism industry by the year 2005. High-level representatives, such as the Director of the United Nations Environment Programme, the Co-ordinator of World Decade for Cultural Development (UNESCO), a Global Program Manager of the World Bank Group, and the Chairman and President of the World Travel and Tourism Council, reported on the ideas and initiatives for sustainable tourism emanating from their respective organizations. Possibly one of the most potentially significant of these is the Green Globe scheme.[25] Newly established by the WTTC and therefore representing the travel industry itself, it is now showing recognition of the need for new endeavour in, and better management of, tourism. At the Conference, the need was clearly shown to be understood that a greater and more equable balance must be achieved between the visitor and the visited, in order to minimize tourism's damaging downside and for the full realization of tourism's many beneficial elements (see also Chapter 3.4). Speaking at a Conference session, the President of IIPT, Louis d' Amore, reminded his audience of the pertinent Marshall McLuhan opinion that on 'spaceship earth. . . . There are no more passengers, only crew'.[26]

The time must be coming when, as was called for at the Conference, a cost/benefit analysis is done when considering whether a tourism development should proceed. Assessment should not be by just financial criteria, but by evaluation of the impact of tourism upon a site in social, cultural and environmental terms. The costs and benefits of tourism can be each of these and more. The time is surely fast approaching when it will be the norm for the impact from tourism to be not only evaluated by all these criteria, and others too probably, but also for the 'polluter' (if he is allowed to proceed with his endeavour) to be made to make suitable recompense for any destructive or damaging elements it may have.

Such procedures represent good management. My message in this book is that we cannot afford *not* to manage cultural tourism better. While we may have a theoretical right to visit a cultural site, in the overall interest it may be necessary that we choose not to exercise that right, at some times and in some places. Then, when it is appropriate in all the circumstances and we *do* go to a cultural site, by positive and appropriate management, not merely luck, there will be that most joyous conjunction, a happy heritage visit. All together, better can we be managing quality cultural tourism.

Issues and questions

* Authenticity.
* Tourism: volume increase and range, extension and alteration.
* Action in concert.
* Sustainability.
* Level of access to sites.
* Europe still a major destination.

a) What are some of the main circumstances of cultural tourism today?
b) What are some of the initiatives under way with a view to developing tourism in a suitable way for the future?
c) Has cultural tourism the capacity to be managed appropriately to meet the needs of the tourist, the presenter and the site?
d) What are useful mechanisms for managing cultural tourism appropriately?

Further reading

Boniface, P. and Fowler, P. J., *Heritage and Tourism in 'the global village'*, London, Routledge, 1993.
Prematilleke, P. L. (ed.), International Scientific Symposium 10th General Assembly Sri Lanka, *Cultural Tourism*, Colombo, ICOMOS, 1993.
Issues of the USA magazine, *Wired*, and from March 1995 of the UK edition.

Glossary

EEC   European Economic Community
EU   European Union
ICOM   International Council on Museums
ICOMOS   International Council on Monuments and Sites
Tourism
   agri   having relation to farms or agriculture
   business   work-related travel, conference attendance, etc.
   cultural   relating to humankind and its life styles and artefacts, those of the past most particularly
   eco   harmonious, sustainable, low-impact
   farm   accommodation in former farmhouses or other buildings of a farm complex
   green   friendly to the natural environment or similar to eco (see above)

   rural   in countryside areas
   social   for low income, or other disabled or disadvantaged group travel markets
UNESCO   United Nations Educational, Scientific and Cultural Organisation
   MAB   Man and Biosphere
UNEP   United Nations Environment Programme
World Heritage Convention   UNESCO agreement of 16 November 1972 to protect the world cultural and natural heritage, producing the designation of World Heritage Sites
World Heritage List   List of World Heritag Sites
World Heritage Site   Site so designated by UNESCO and featuring on the World Heritage List
WTO   World Tourism Organization
WTTC   World Travel and Tourism Council

Notes

Part 1 Introduction

1.1 The situation of cultural tourism

1 As reported in *The Guardian*, 25 March 1992, p. 15.
2 Sudjic, D., *The 100 Mile City*, London, Deutsch, 1992, p. 264.
3 In *UNESCOPRESSE*, Vol. 2, No. 19, 22 May 1992.
4 Preface of Ascher, F., *Tourism: Transnational Corporations and Cultural Identities*, Paris, UNESCO, 1985.
5 Rogers, R., *Architecture: A Modern View*, London and New York, Thames & Hudson, 1990, 1991 and 1992, p. 9.
6 ibid., p. 27.
7 Rhampal, S., *Our Country, The Planet: Forging a Partnership for Survival*, London, Lime Tree, 1992.
8 Ignatieff, M., 'We're no angels if we foul our nest', *The Observer*, 7 June 1992, p. 25.
9 Wood, K. and House, S., *The Good Tourist: A Worldwide Guide for the Green Traveller*, London, Mandarin, 1991, p. 9.
10 Ashcroft, P., in *Green Tourism: A Training Seminar for European Rangers, Warders and Interpreters*, Peak Park Joint Planning Board, 1991, p. 2.
11 ibid., p. 3.
12 ibid.
13 Ignatieff, M., 'Bread and circuses won't do, David', *The Observer*, 12 July 1992, p. 21.
14 Aslet, C., 'The hit list that threatens our national heritage', *The Mail on Sunday*, 1 November 1992, p. 19.
15 Adair, G., *The Post-Modernist Always Rings Twice: Reflections on Culture in the 90s*, London, Fourth Estate, 1992, p. 3.
16 Boniface, P. and Fowler, P. J., *Heritage and Tourism in 'the global village'*, London, Routledge, 1993, p. 4.
17 Pugh, D., 'Islamic militants threaten tourists', *The Guardian*, 29 August 1992, p. 8.
18 Welsh, E., 'Terror threat hits Egypt tours', *Weekend Telegraph*, 7 November 1992, p.XXI.
19 Pugh, op. cit.
20 ibid.
21 Report, *Tourism and the Environment: Maintaining The Balance*, London, English Tourist Board and the Employment Department Group, 1991, p. 47.

Part 2 Components

2.1 The user

1 Thoreau, H. D., *Walden*, Ticknor & Fields, 1854; Princeton, Princeton University Press, 1971, 1973, p. 8.
2 For example, Laws, E., quoting Blazey, Crompton, Goodrich, Holloway, among others, in his *Tourism Marketing: Service and Quality Management Perspectives*, Cheltenham, Stanley Thornes (Publishers) Ltd, 1991,Chapter 4, and Pearce, D., quoting Gray, Iso-Ahola and Opinion Research Corporation in his *Tourism Today: A Geographical Analysis*, Harlow and New York, Longman, 1987, Chapter 2.
3 Koubska, L., *Lidové Noviny*, report in *The Guardian*, 19 June 1992, p. 24.
4 Forrest, E., 'Reading books is not worth the effort', reprint of *Spectator* article in *The Sunday Times*, 21 March 1992, News Review, p. 2.
5 Frean, A., 'Haven to end agony of the dancing bears' in *The European*, 18–21 June 1992, p. 3. See also Rugman, J., 'Last grim waltz for

the dancing bears', *The Observer*, 3 October 1993, p. 20.

6 Fisher, P., 'From virtual reality to virtual insanity', *The Guardian*, 11 June 1992, p. 31.

7 *The European*, 4–7 March 1993, p. 25.

8 See Deedes, W. F., 'Another Country', *The Daily Telegraph* Weekend, 18 April 1992.

9 Horne, D., *The Great Museum*, London, Pluto, 1984, p. 10.

10 ibid., p. 11.

11 See Chippindale, C. (ed.) *et al.*, *Who Owns Stonehenge*, London, Batsford, 1991; Fowler, P. J., *The Past in Contemporary Society: Then, Now*, London and New York, Routledge, 1992; Golding, F., chapter in Cleere, H. (ed.), *Archaeological Heritage Management in the Modern World*, One World Archaeology series, London, Unwin Hyman (now Routledge), 1989, pp. 256–64.

12 *The European*, 12–15 November 1992, p. 45.

13 Sudjic, D., 'A nation ready for take-off', *The Guardian*, 6 April 1992, p. 38.

14 See article in the American *W* magazine, 27 April–4 May 1992, pp. 20, 22.

15 National Railway Museum, York, leaflet, undated.

16 Christiansen, R., 'A thousand arts for a thousand trades', *The Observer*, 22 November 1992, p. 57.

17 Rogers, R., *Architecture: A Modern View*, London, Thames & Hudson, 1991, p. 15.

18 Urry, J., *The Tourist Gaze: Leisure and Travel in Contemporary Societies*, London, Sage, 1990, p. 4.

19 Harding, I., 'Taking the yen out of Paris', *The European*, 7–10 May 1992, p. 3.

20 Harlow, J., 'Capital cover-up hides Albert from tourist eyes', *The Sunday Times*, 9 August 1992, p. 5.

21 Ivy, M., 'Hidden treasures blink in the light', *The European*, 21–24 May 1992, p. 22.

22 Radford, T., 'Story of crowded capital creates display problem', *The Guardian*, 2 September 1992, p. 5.

2.2 The presenter

1 Rogers, R., *Architecture: A Modern View*, London, Thames & Hudson, 1991, p. 9.

2 Eckstein, J. (ed.), *Cultural Trends 1992*, Issue 14, Vol. 4, No. 2, Policy Studies Institute, 1992, Conclusion, p. 60.

3 Sutton, H., 'Time for tourism to discover its own place in the sun', *The European*, 11–14 June 1992, p. 40.

4 Davis, W., 'The tourist industry deserves a break', *The Observer*, 3 January 1993, p. 19.

5 Redgrave, R., 'A South Sea Tale', Voyages Jules Verne Serenissima Travel, *Travel Review*, February 1992, p. 15.

6 Barry Parker in his presentation in a session at the IIPT Global Conference, 'Building a Sustainable World Through Tourism', in 1994.

7 Report in *The Daily Yomiuri*, 25 February 1993, p. 15.

8 Paterson, T., 'Dresden catches up with its past', *The European*, 25–28 February 1994, p. 6.

9 Hopkins, A., 'Across the Wall and into the trees', *The European*, 23–26 July 1992, p. 11.

10 Reid, M., 'Riches that have yet to lure the Europeans', *The Guardian*, 20 July 1992, p. 9.

11 Coles, J., 'National Heritage museum judges vote Man an island in a class unto itself', *The Guardian*, 8 July 1992, p. 4.

12 See McAlpine, A., 'Packed lunch and parsimony is what a gondolier hates', *The European*, 12–15 November 1992, p. 12.

13 Crawshaw, J., 'Out of the purple haze', *The European*, 19–22 November 1992, p. 27.

14 Harding, I., 'Catholics go into battle over sale of historic abbey', *The European*, 4–7 June 1992, p. 42.

15 Report in *The Japan Times*, 20 February 1993, p. 2.

16 Davis, M., *City of Quartz: Excavating the Future in Los Angeles*, London, Verso, 1990; Vintage, 1992, p. 111.

17 Willey, D., 'Saintly bankers enter the Colosseum arena', *The Observer*, 21 June 1992, p. 15.

18 Harrison, D., 'Dangers undermining the city of Bath', *The Observer*, 22 November 1992, p. 13.

19 *Daily Mail*, 23 April 1992, p. 21.

20 Centre for Environmental Interpretation's Introduction to English Heritage, *Visitors Welcome*, London, HMSO, 1988, p. 2.

21 ibid., p. 3.

22 Davidson, R., *Tourism in Europe*, London and Paris, Pitman, Longman and Techniplus, 1992.

23 Hudson, K., *Museums of Influence*, Cambridge, Cambridge University Press, 1987, p. 160.

24 MacCannell, D., *Empty Meeting Grounds: The Tourist Papers*, London and New York, Routledge, 1992, p. 31.

25 Woollacott, M., 'When the death of a tourist meets the death of a dream', *The Guardian*, 14 April 1993, p. 18.

2.3 The item

1 UNESCO, 'Convention for the Protection of the World Cultural and Natural Heritage', 16 November 1972, 1. Definitions of the Cultural Heritage, Article 1.
2 ibid., introductory remarks.
3 M'Bow, A.-M., Foreword in UNESCO, *A Legacy for All: The World's Major Cultural and Historic Sites*, Paris, UNESCO, 1982.
4 Phillips, A., in the Report of the Conference, *Tourism, Recreation and Conservation*, Peak Park Joint Planning Board, 1985, p. 5.
5 Burrell, T., in ibid., p. 70.
6 Currie, R. R. and Var, T., in Tabata, R., Cherem, G. and Yamashiro, J. (eds), Proceedings of the Heritage Interpretation International Third Global Congress, *Joining Hands for Quality Tourism: Interpretation, Preservation and the Travel Industry*, Honolulu, University of Hawaii, 1992, p. 75.
7 Report in UNESCO, *Sources*, No. 39, July–August 1992, p. 15.
8 West B., in Lumley, R. (ed.), *The Museum Time-Machine*, London and New York, Routledge, 1988, p. 54.
9 ibid., p. 55.
10 Leaflet, *The World Heritage*, Madrid, UNESCO, 1992.
11 Vuillamy, E., 'Sights for Sour Eyes', *The Guardian*, 21 October 1992, p. 5.
12 Evans, K., 'Battle royal over repairs to shrine', *The Guardian*, 16 June 1992, p. 10.
13 In *UNESCOPRESSE*, Vol. 2, No. 20, 29 May 1992.
14 Kennedy, M., 'The bear necessities of life', *Weekend Guardian*, 21–22 March 1992, p. 25.
15 Troev, T., 'Tourists tread on thin ice in Polar wastes', *The European*, 30 April–3 May 1992, p. 16.
16 North West Water leaflet, undated.
17 Pommery, C., 'The tourist boom we don't really want', *The European*, 25–28 June 1992, p. 24.
18 *Daily Mail*, 21 November 1992, p. 55.
19 Wainwright, M., 'Moorland hikers invited to tread new path through Cleveland's dead souls', *The Guardian*, 19 December 1992, p. 5.
20 Suraiya, J., 'Troubled times in high places', *Weekend Guardian*, 23–24 May 1992, p. 22.
21 Hopkins, A., 'Where the knives are out for tourists', *Weekend Telegraph*, 6 June 1992, p. XXIV
22 Jones, T., 'Going gets tough as turf gets going',

The Journal, 22 April 1993, p. 20.
23 Lamb, R., 'Booking in for green dreams', *The Sunday Times*, 22 March 1992, p. 16.

Part 3 Objectives

3.1 Attracting

1 For a depiction of the Pompidou Centre's publics, see Heinich, N. (translated Turner, C.) in Lumley, R. (ed.), *The Museum Time Machine*, London and New York, Routledge, 1988, p. 205.
2 Reported in *WTO News: Tourism Policy Trends and Perspectives*, No. 8, September 1992, p. 5.
3 Reported in *Bradford's Yorkshire Travel News*, Special 10th Anniversary Issue.
4 McIvor, A., 'The Spain that tourism forgot', *The European*, 14–17 May 1992, p. 11.
5 Yates, R., 'Gissa job ... in the movies', *The Observer*, 13 June 1992, p. 55.
6 Report in *The European*, 17–20 December 1992, p. 42.
7 Brunton, J., 'Would you mind if I took over your tomb?', *The European*, 22–25 July 1993, p. 18.
8 Hussell, L., 'Marseille cleans up its act', *The European*, 22–25 October 1992, p. 38.
9 Sudjic, D., 'A place to hang out', *The Guardian*, 15 March 1993.
10 Arpin, R., 'Museums in France poised for their role in the new Europe', *Forces*, No. 98, Summer 1992, p. 82.
11 Cossens, N., in *Seminar on New Forms of Demand, New Products*, Madrid, WTO, ?1991, p. 110.
12 Buscall, E., 'France still top as tourism set to soar', *The European*, 22–25 October 1992, p. 4.
13 Elliott, H., 'Tourism trumpets buoyant message', *The Times*, 20 November 1992, p. 9.

3.2 Detracting

1 Pearman, H., 'Suburban development', *The Sunday Times*, 6 September 1992, 8, p. 4.
2 Wright, P., 'Keeping the hills alive', *The Guardian*, 19 August 1994, pp. 10–11.
3 Weller, R., (of Associated Press), 'Highway 40 is road to extinction of Dinosaur', *The Independent*, 10 July 1993, p. 1.
4 Neale, G., 'Tourists "Killing the Alps" ', *Weekend Telegraph*, 3 October 1992, p. XXIX.

5 Brady, D., 'The ice men cometh', *The Guardian Weekend*, 19 June 1993, p. 57.
6 Ingrams, R., in *The Observer*, 18 October 1992, p. 22.

3.3 Educating and informing

1 Pearman, H., 'Survival of the slickest', *The Sunday Times*, 26 July 1992, 7, p. 12.
2 Rheingold, H., *Virtual Reality*, London, Secker & Warburg, 1991; London, Mandarin, 1992, p. 250.
3 Hewison, R., 'Show business', *The Sunday Times*, 24 January 1993, 8, p. 9.
4 Porritt, J. and Winner, D., *The Coming of the Greens*, London, Fontana, 1988, p. 112.
5 Thomas, S., 'Future of the past', *The Guardian*, 23 June 1992, p. 23.
6 Reported in *The European*, 23–26 July 1992, p. 5.
7 Brochure *le patrimoine mondial/World Heritage*, Canadian Parks Service and Environment Canada undated, p. 1.
8 Rona-Beaulieu, S. and Janin, S., 'For lots of us, museum rhymes with humdrum' in UNESCO, *Museum*, No. 1, 1992, pp. 40–4.
9 Pearman, op. cit.
10 See McClellan, J., 'Lost in cyberspace', *The Observer*, 14 November 1993, pp. 4–5; Millar, P., 'Taking leave of your senses', *The Sunday Times*, 26 September 1993, 9, pp. 2–3; Short, D., 'Exploring the real world of virtual Reality', *The European*, 28 January–3 Febuary 1994, p. 21.
11 Cotton, B. and Oliver, R., *Understanding Hypermedia: From Multimedia to Virtual Reality*, London, Phaidon, 1993, p. 121.
12 Boniface, P. and Fowler, P. J., op. cit., p. 161, and Rheingold, H., ibid.
13 *Guardian Education*, 15 June 1993, p. 16.
14 Cotton and Brown, op. cit., p. 88.
15 Sulaiman, S., 'Toys for the grown-up boys', *The Guardian*, 23 June 1992, p. 16.
16 Lesgards, R., in his Introduction to the *Guide to the Permanent Exhibition Explora*, la villette cité des Sciences et de l'Industrie and Aubin Imperimeur, Ligugé-Poitiers, 1990, p. 3.

3.4 Entertaining

1 Weber, P., 'Glance macabre' article from *Le Soir* in *The Guardian*, 17 July 1992, p. 26.
2 Pearman, H., 'More frolics than relics', *The Sunday Times*, 31 May 1992, 7, p. 13.

3.5 Commercializing

1 Edmonds, M., 'Slums and sleaze for all', *Weekend Telegraph*, 7 March 1992, p. VIII.
2 Leedham, R., 'Last of the big pesetas' report (accompanying a report by Edwards, M., 'Adios Eldorado'), *The Sunday Times*, 4 July 1993, 9, p. 25.
3 Sullivan, R., 'Museums "need a renaissance"', *The European*, 3–6 December 1992, p. 38.
4 Spinks, P., 'Van Gogh bails out Mondrian as Dutch slash arts subsidies', *The Guardian*, 17 June 1992, p. 7.
5 Usborne, D., 'Vermont set to fight the mega-store predators', *The Independent*, 10 July 1993, p. 12.

Part 4 Conclusion

4.1 Cultural tourism now and for the future

1 Balmer, D., 'Green go-getters may be tourist wizards of Oz', *The Observer*, 17 May 1992, p. 61.
2 *The Sunday Times*, 31 May 1991, 1, pp. 12–13.
3 Rocha, J., 'Environment superpower role for Japan', *The Guardian*, 5 June 1991, p. 8.
4 Savignac, A. E., in *WTO News: Tourism Policy Trends and Perspectives*, No. 7, July/August 1992, p. 1.
5 Davidson, R., *Tourism in Europe*, London, Pitman, and Longman and Techniplus, 1992, p. 3.
6 Ignatieff, M., 'Stones of Sarajevo put us to shame', *The Observer*, 17 May 1992, p. 19.
7 Millar, P., 'Everybody's castle', *The European*, 26–9 November 1994, p. 9.
8 Battersby, D., 'Learning to cope with tourism boom', *The European*, 19–27 March 1992, p. 18.
9 Ward, J., 'Tourism depends on trained people', *The Journal*, 20 May 1992, p. 51.
10 Reported in Rheingold, H., *Virtual Reality*, London, Secker & Warburg, 1991; London, Mandarin, 1992, p. 291.
11 Reported by Wesker, A., in 'The artist and the gatekeeper', *The Guardian*, 27 October 1992, p. 4.
12 Yong-Boon Yeo, G., 'Cultures in competition', *International Herald Tribune*, Tokyo Edition, 18 February 1993, p. 4.
13 Winchester, S., *The Pacific*, London, Hutchinson, 1991; London, Arrow, 1992, p. 440.

14 Sudjic, D., 'Of arches and arch-enemies', *The Guardian*, 29 March 1993, p. 5.

15 Coupland, D., *Generation X: Tales for an Accelerated Culture*, St Martin's Press, 1991; London, Abacus, 1992, p. 11.

16 Roden, C., 'Gameboys and girls stay in to play', *The Guardian*, 13 April 1993, p. 11.

17 Report, 'Super Intelligent Logic System Developed' in *The Daily Yomiuri*, 25 February, 1993, p. 3.

18 Ashihara, Y., *Kakureta chisujo*, Tokyo, Chuokoron-sha, 1986, then published as *The Hidden Order: Tokyo through the Twentieth Century*, Tokyo and New York, Kodansha, 1989, p. 63.

19 Savignac, A. E., in *WTO News: Tourism Policy Trends and Perspectives*, No. 7, op. cit.

20 Ashihara, op. cit., p. 121.

21 *The Daily Yomiuri*, 25 February 1993, p. 3.

22 Coupland, D., *Shampoo Planet*, Pocket Books, 1992; London, Simon & Schuster, 1993, p. 9.

23 Ishihara, S., *The Japan That Can Say No*, New York, Simon & Schuster, 1989, p. 100.

24 *Code of Ethics and Guidelines for Sustainable Tourism*, Tourism Industry Association of Canada and National Round Table on the Environment and the Economy, undated ?1994.

25 Green Globe, 'A worldwide environmental program for the Travel and Tourism industry', the initial scheme of which was launched in 1994. The Green Globe office is at 4 Suffolk Place, London W1Y 4BS.

26 McLuhan, M. and Powers, B. R., *The Global Village: Transformations in World Life and Media in the 21st Century*, New York, Oxford University Press, 1989; Oxford, Oxford University Press, 1992, p. 98.

Select bibliography

This Select Bibliography represents a short general list of publications whose concern in one way or another is tourism. The Select Bibliography should augment those lists provided in the References, and the Further Reading which is located at the end of each chapter. Some publications appearing in the Select Bibliography will also feature in a chapter's lists of references and Further Reading.

General

Fladmark, F. M. (ed.), *Cultural Tourism*, London, Donhead, 1994.

Pearce, D. G. and Butler, R. W. (eds), *Tourism Research: Critiques and Challenges*, London, Routledge, in association with the International Academy for the Study of Tourism, 1992.

Prematilleke, P. L. (ed.), International Scientific Symposium 10th General Assembly Sri Lanka, *Cultural Tourism*, Colombo, ICOMOS, 1993.

Turner, L. and Ash, J., *The Golden Hordes: International Tourism and the Pleasure Periphery*, London, Constable, 1975. (Extraordinarily far-sighted, describing and depicting tourism with great perspicacity and clarity.)

Ward, J., Higson P. and Campbell, W., *GNVQ Advanced Leisure and Tourism*, Cheltenham, Stanley Thornes (Publishers) Ltd/GNVQ, 1994.

Management methods and approaches

Anfield, J., 'Loving them to death: sustainable tourism in National Parks', in Fladmark, J. M. (ed.), *Cultural Tourism*, London, Donhead, 1994, pp. 199–207.

Berenbaum, M., 'About the museum', in *The World Must Know: The History of the Holocaust as Told in the United States Holocaust Memorial Museum*, New York, Little Brown & Company, 1993, pp. 233–5.

Centre for Environmental Interpretation, *Visitors Welcome*, English Heritage, London, HMSO, 1988.

Commission on the European Community, *Community Action Plan to Assist Tourism*, April 1991.

Council for the Protection of Rural England, *Leisure Landscapes – Leisure, Culture and the English Countryside*, London, CPRE, 1994.

Frayling, C., *The Face of Tutankhamun*, London and Boston, Faber & Faber, 1992. (Many of the crucial issues relating to cultural heritage management, more especially in the context of tourism, were raised in the final programme, broadcast on 18 December 1992, of Professor Christopher Frayling's BBC 2 series *The Face of Tutankhamun*. The above book accompanies the series.)

Guidelines: Development of National Parks and Protected Areas for Tourism, Madrid, WTO, 1992.

Hetherington, A., Inskeep, E. and McIntyre, G., *Sustainable Tourism Development: Guide for Local Planners*, Madrid, WTO/UNEP, 1992.

Lea, J., *Tourism and Development in the Third World*, London, Routledge, 1988, p. 27.

Report, *Tourism Carrying Capacity*, Madrid, WTO/UNEP, 1992.

Tabata, R., Yamashiro, J. and Cherem, G. (eds) Proceedings of the Heritage Intepretation International Third Global Congress, *Joining Hands for Quality Tourism: Interpretation, Preservation and the Travel Industry*, Honolulu, University of Hawaii, 1992.

Tourism Concern for the World Wide Fund for Nature, *Beyond the Green Horizon*, 1992.

Tourism Industry Association of Canada and National Round Table on the Environment and the Economy, *Code of Ethics and Guidelines for Sustainable Tourism*, undated ?1994

Vergo, P. (ed.), *The New Museology*, London, Reaktion, 1989, pp. 64–5, 70–1, 72–3, 146–7, 170–1.

Womack, J.P., Jones, D.T., and Roos, D., *The Machine That Changed The World*, New York, Rawson Associates, and Toronto, Collier Macmillan Canada, 1990.

Among useful publications in general are: the *One World Archaeology* series, London, formerly Unwin Hyman, now Routledge. See, for example, Cleere, H. (ed.), *Archaeological Heritage Management in the Modern World*; issues of the National Trust *Education Supplement*; the UNESCO magazine *Sources*; *WTO News*.

Overall context

Naisbitt, J. and Aburdene P., *Megatrends 2000*, London, Sidgwick & Jackson, 1990.

Ohmae, K., *The Borderless World: Power and Strategy in the Interlinked Economy*, London, Collins, 1990; London, Fontana, 1992.

Toffler, A., *Powershift: Knowledge, Wealth and Violence at the End of the 21st Century*, New York, Bantam, 1990.

Technology

Cotton, B. and Oliver, R., *Understanding Hypermedia: From Multimedia to Virtual Reality*, London, Phaidon, 1993.

Kurokawa, K., *Rediscovering Japanese Space*, New York and Tokyo, Weatherhill, 1988, p. 24.

Rheingold, H., *The Virtual Community: Finding Connection In A Computerised World*, London, Secker & Warburg, 1994.

Woolley, B., *Virtual Worlds: A Journey in Hype and Hyperreality*, Oxford, Blackwell, 1992; London, Penguin, 1993.

The item

Ashworth, G. J. and Tunbridge, J. E., *The Tourist-Historic City*, London and New York, Belhaven, 1990. (This covers the city in relation to tourism. In their Preface the authors state that 'the city at the end at the twentieth century was increasingly exploiting historicity as a contemporary resource, particularly in response to a growing demand in society for the phenomenon we call the tourist-historic city. We believe that this has already set a course for the city in the twenty-first century.')

Cleere, H. (ed.), *Archaeological Heritage Management in the Modern World*, London, in the *One World Archaeology* series, formerly Unwin Hyman, now Routledge, 1989, pp. 2–3, and on Stonehenge specifically, Golding, F., pp. 259–61.

Currie, R. R. and Var, T., 'Nature- and historic-based tourism', in Tabata, R., Yamashiro, J. and Cherem, G. (eds), Proceedings of the Heritage Interpretation International Third Global Congress, *Joining Hands for Quality Tourism: Interpretation Preservation and the Travel Industry*, Honolulu, University of Hawaii, 1992, p. 75.

UNESCO, *A Legacy for All*, Paris, UNESCO, 1982.

The tourist

Davidson, R., *Tourism in Europe*, London and Paris, Pitman, Longman and Techniplus, 1992.

Davies, M., *City of Quartz: Excavating the Future in Los Angeles*, Verso, 1990; London, Vintage, 1992, p. 111.

Frommer, A. B., *The New World of Travel*, New York, Prentice Hall Press, 1988. (For signs of a newly emerging viewpoint entering the tourism mainstream.)

Horne, D., *The Intelligent Tourist*, McMahons Point, New South Wales, Margaret Gee Publishing, 1992.

Pearce, P. L., *The Social Psychology of Tourist Behaviour*, Oxford, Pergamon, 1982.

WTO Seminar in Nicosia, Cyprus, 8–9 May 1991, Proceedings, *Seminar on New Forms of Demand. New Products*, Madrid, WTO, 1991.

For consideration of some tourist motivations, see Laws, E., *Tourism Marketing; Service and Quality Management Perspectives*, Cheltenham, Stanley Thornes (Publishers) Ltd, 1991, Chapters 4–6; Pearce, D., *Tourism Today: A Geographical Analysis*, Harlow and New York, Longman, 1987, especially pp. 22–3; Pearce, P. L., *The Social Psychology of Tourist Behaviour*, Oxford, Pergamon Press, 1982, especially p. 65. and pp. 128–9; Ryan, C., *Recreational Tourism: A Social Science Perspective*, London and New York, Routledge, 1991.

World Heritage

Feilden, B. and Jokilehto, J., Management Guidelines for World Cultural Heritage Sites, Rome, ICCROM/UNESCO/ICOMOS, 1993.

Issues of *The World Heritage Newsletter*, Paris, The World Heritage Centre, UNESCO.

Map of World Heritage Sites in the leaflet *The World Heritage*, Madrid, UNESCO, 1992.

Masterworks of Man and Nature: Preserving our World Heritage, Patonga, Harper-MacRae Publishing Pty Limited, 1992.

Pieris, S. and Prematilleke, P. L. (eds), *Cultural Tourism: Tourism at World Heritage Cultural Sites: The Site Manager's Handbook*, Colombo, Sri Lanka National Committee of ICOMOS for ICOMOS, 1993.

Index

124

Printed in the United Kingdom
by Lightning Source UK Ltd.
136374UK00013B/1/A